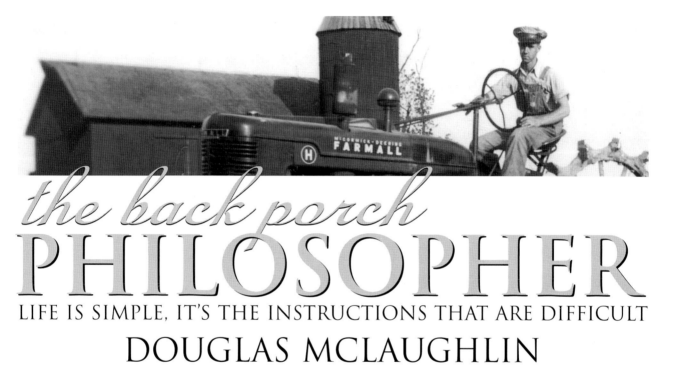

the back porch
PHILOSOPHER

LIFE IS SIMPLE, IT'S THE INSTRUCTIONS THAT ARE DIFFICULT

DOUGLAS MCLAUGHLIN

The
Guest
Cottage Inc.
dba Amherst Press

Dedication
To my wife Sharon, I thank you and I love you.

Published By:
The Guest Cottage, Inc.
8821 Hwy 47
PO Box 848
Woodruff, WI 54568
E-mail: info@theguestcottage.com
Website: www.theguestcottage.com

Designed By:
Carole E. Sauers

To request a catalog of other publications by The Guest Cottage,
please call 1-800-333-8122

Index

INTRODUCTION 5

KEEP IT SIMPLE, STUPID 10

SIMPLE IS AS SIMPLE DOES 19

THE SIMPLE TRUTH IS 30

PACK JUST ENOUGH BAGGAGE FOR A SIMPLE TRIP 38

LOVE IS SO SIMPLE 47

PURE AND SIMPLE 60

SIMPLE SIMON 72

IS SIMPLE ENOUGH 86

KEEP IT SIMPLE 98

TO ASK THE SIMPLE QUESTION IS HARD 109

SUMMARY 125

CONCLUSION 127

This book started out as a discussion between my son and me on the meaning and origins of different clichés. What finally evolved was a philosophy on life—albeit, a very simple philosophy. It's not intended to be the latest in a very long and illustrious study of philosophy. I only wish that were the case! It became clear to me during the writing of this book that each of us needs to become our own philosopher. We need to know what makes us tick. We need to know why we behave the way we do. We need to know what our passion is. The only way you can achieve that honorable goal is by thinking. Thinking will allow you to arrive at your own solutions and conclusions. When you have done that, you can call yourself a philosopher.

It was a bitterly cold, snowy and wind-blown evening in early January when I told my son that it was, "Cold enough to freeze the balls off a brass monkey." Needless to say, he laughed and agreed with me. He then said he had never seen a brass monkey. "Where should I go to see one, at the zoo, on the top of a flagpole or at a bar?" I laughed with him and explained that he would have to go back to the days of the sailing ships in order to see one. He didn't know what I was talking about! A brass monkey was a small cart made of brass that held the ship's cannon balls. When the temperature was cold enough, the brass cart would start to contract and the cannon balls would roll off the "brass monkey." It was evident from my son's question that the actual meaning of the brass monkey and its balls had been lost.

My son started asking me about other ancient clichés and their actual meanings. I told him about, "not worth a tinkers damn," "mad as a hatter" and "keep your power dry." We continued on with other well-used clichés such as, "where there's smoke, there's fire," "don't count your chickens before they hatch" and "two wrongs don't make a right." We asked one another what we thought each cliché meant. Most of the time, our views were not similar.

It was about this time that I remembered an incident from my son's past concerning an electric fence. My son finally agreed with me. "Well, wonders never cease!" I proceeded to make up a brand-new cliché, "never pee on an electric fence." My son remembered the electric fence episode. He was only three or four years old when he did pee on an electric fence, and it made a lasting impression on him! He mentioned, "It was quite a shock to me!" We started laughing again.

It was at this point that my son said, "I just thought of a new cliché: 'Never open a window on an airplane.'"

I immediately agreed with him and told him to "never write a check with no money in the bank." My son actually agreed with me for the second time.

This senseless discussion between father and son went on for another 30 minutes with each of us trying to out-do the other with brand-new, original and worthwhile clichés. We chuckled, laughed and generally agreed on our high level of intelligence. We determined that we were both brilliantly sarcastic and, at the same time, very clever. It was a fun evening!

The next day was Sunday and instead of paying attention to the church services, I was looking up Bible clichés. A few of the Bible verses I found were: "turn the other cheek," "do unto others as you would have them do unto you," "there is nothing new under the sun," "an eye for an eye and a tooth for a tooth," "seek and you shall find" and "money is the root of all evil." I decided that one of the qualifications for writing gospel was knowing a good cliché when you see one.

6

During the next few weeks, I recounted the evening's narrative and the Bible verses with many of my friends. They surprised me!

First, nobody knew what the frozen brass monkey meant. I wasn't surprised that they didn't know the literal meaning, but I was astonished at the many different explanations they gave me. One friend actually thought brass monkeys were a species of extinct Asian monkeys!

Second, not all clichés mean the same thing to all people. This was certainly true with the brass monkey and its balls. It was also true of many other sayings. I started asking people the meaning of well-known clichés. I also asked for their interpretations of clichés such as: "the grass is not always greener on the other side," "it takes one to know one" and "what goes up must come down." I even threw in a few of my son's homemade clichés for good measure. Almost everyone I talked to had contrary ideas concerning each cliché's message.

Third, the meaning can be lost over time, as evidenced by the brass monkey. The meaning can also change with the passage of time.

Fourth, new clichés are being added all the time. My son and I proved that by making up a few ourselves. Ours aren't well known yet, but you can never tell.

There was one answer, however, that I received every time I asked what a particular cliché meant. "I don't know" was the most common answer. Whenever I heard, "I don't know," I would not accept it. There was more than one friend who became irritable at my incessant questioning. Because of the answers I heard, I "jumped to a conclusion." The conclusion I jumped to was that most people will not, could not or would not take the time to understand the cliché's message. They wanted someone else to tell them what it meant. They wanted someone else to think for them.

7

According to the media, we are in the throes of a worldwide spiritual re-awakening. How can we awake from a deep sleep if we don't know what we think? In order to be awake spiritually, you must also be awake in other areas of your psyche. Are we to accept what others tell us is right and wrong? Are we going to follow without question? Are we going to explore only one avenue to a spiritual rebirth? I hope your answer is no!

Maybe, just maybe, we need to become eclectic during our journey to truth. Each of us was put here to grow, learn and teach. By far the best way to begin the journey of growing, learning and teaching is to know yourself first. This means you should know why you believe as you do in all aspects of life, not only the spiritual. "All are not saints that go to church." Certainly not only the physical world. "Man cannot live by bread alone."

The following list consists of contrasting clichés. Which ones do you believe are true, and why?

"Absence makes the heart grow fonder," vs. "Out of sight, out of mind."

"Variety is the spice of life," vs. "Don't change horses in mid-stream."

"The customer is always right," vs. "Let the buyer beware."

"Children are poor's men's riches," vs. "Wife and children are bills of charges."

8

"Nothing ventured, nothing gained," vs. "If you play with fire, you get burnt."

"Delays are dangerous," vs. "If today will not, tomorrow may."

"Bread is the staff of life," vs. "Man cannot live by bread alone."

I decided that since new clichés are being added each day, why not add some of my own? I also decided that since I was the one who was adding the new clichés, I should be the one who told the masses what they meant. Feel free to change the meaning of the new clichés if you want. The only thing I ask is for you to think before you answer. By thinking and answering the above, you have taken that first step on the road to being a back porch philosopher. At the very least, you've started thinking! As we all know, thinking leads to understanding.

This is not an attempt to solve the world's problems. It's not an attempt to solve your problems. It is, however, an attempt to cause you to think. By thinking, maybe we can solve some of our problems. We have more time to think than our ancestors did. We need to use that time productively. Our prodigies will thank us for the endeavor. After all, we are the baby boomers!

I hope you have as much fun reading this very simple, plain and unimportant book on the philosophy of life as I did striving to produce it.

9

Keep It Simple, Stupid

"Out of clutter, find simplicity."—*Albert Einstein*

Most things in life are simple, it's the instructions that are difficult!

I'm reminded of what Mr. Spock would say in Star Trek, "Live long and prosper." That, my dear friends, is a great thought! Do you have any idea how we can do that?

When I was a child, I was positive I wanted to go to heaven. It sounded like a neat place, full of angels, ice cream and a neverending game of baseball! Heaven was mine for the asking; all I had to do was live a long and fruitful life and die. Then I found out that if I wanted to go to heaven, I couldn't eat meat on Fridays and had to go to church every Sunday plus seven other holy days that were the same as Sunday. The holy days were worse because you had to go to the early mass at 6:30 a.m.

If I did eat meat on Friday or miss church on purpose, I'd go straight to hell. I couldn't pass go or collect $200. But if my sins weren't on purpose—like I just forgot it was Friday, or my folks forgot to have me baptized—there was another place for me to reside and that place was "limbo." Limbo was almost the same as heaven, but not quite. You couldn't visit with God, and instead of a neverending game of baseball you only got to play badminton. I certainly didn't think that was any way to treat little kids who died before they were baptized, or ate a hot dog on Friday. But, if you did end up in limbo, you could get out by the prayers of other little kids still on Earth. I was taught that 300 "Our Fathers" would cut a limbo day off for some poor limbo soul! I'm proud to say that during my eighth year of life, I shorted some poor sucker's stay in limbo by exactly 16 hours. I

10

wanted to liberate more limbo souls but an 8-year-old can only stand kneeling and praying for so long! I wonder if there are still some souls serving time in limbo on the Friday meat rap?

It was about this time I started to worry about my best friend Paul, a non-Catholic. I wanted Paul to go to heaven with me because he was a good guy and my best friend. I was informed by the nuns that Paul had hardly any chance of being heaven-bound as he was not Catholic. My reply to the nuns was, "But you said all you had to do was be good." That's when I found out Protestants weren't allowed into heaven unless a Catholic sponsored them. We Catholics were trying to make heaven "by invitation only."

The instructions were starting to get more and more complicated. At about age 14, I discovered girls. Mind you, I still wanted to go to heaven and everybody still told me all I had to do was be good. It was OK to look at girls. But, you couldn't touch them and, heaven forbid, you couldn't have impure thoughts about them. I didn't give a hoot about impure thoughts when I was eight, but by age 14, every other thought was impure. I decided since I couldn't touch or think about girls, I had to do something. That's when I was informed that the something I had in mind was also impure. I was in a heck of a fix. I couldn't think about girls, couldn't touch girls and I couldn't even touch myself. The instructions were really starting to get complicated!

At age 16, I found out we are supposed to be fruitful and multiply, but only with certain people—white Catholic girls. There was not one pretty, white Catholic girl in my entire high school. There was no way I was going to be fruitful and multiply with the white Catholic girls I knew! I guess that was when I decided the instructions were getting out of hand! I knew I wanted to touch, but I couldn't because of the limbo thing. Every time I touched myself, I vigorously added

11

another 17.7 months to my stay in limbo. At last count, I added an additional 969 limbo years with no chance for parole!

I finally graduated from high school with my virtue still intact, much to my chagrin. College was my next great life's adventure. If I thought the instructions were difficult before, the college instructions were quadrupled. We were instructed by older, more experienced college students to drink to excess, engage in sit-ins, get lucky often and go to few classes. The instructions my parents gave me didn't include any of the college instructions. Life was becoming even more complicated!

After college, I got drafted and was expected to shoot at people. I knew the Fifth Commandment said, "Thou shall not kill." Besides that, I wasn't mad at anyone who lived on the other side of the world. I was also very confident that, if I would shoot at those people on the other side of the world, they would probably shoot back at me. That fact didn't hold any appeal to me at all! I still wanted to get to heaven, but it was getting harder and harder. After the Army, I went through the "love, honor and obey" thing, started working, reared children, lost jobs, went through a divorce, experienced the death of loved ones and saw what dramatic effects a tragic accident can do to family life. Life was not getting any easier.

Wise men through the ages have urged us to simplify, simplify, simplify! That is advice worth exploring and living by. I still want to get to heaven. I've decided that my first thought to be good at age eight was the right one. It has taken me 50 years to realize I was a reasonably smart 8-year-old and I plan on being a reasonably wise 50-year-old. I decided not to let the instructions get in the way of being wise and good.

If your life directions are complicated, it's only because you have

12

allowed instructions to get in the way of what is really important in life. Each of us should live by the motto of K.I.S.S. (keep it simple, stupid). So, go out there and become simple-minded!

"You can't please everyone so you got to please yourself."—*Ricky Nelson*
   Always believe in yourself!

If you don't believe in yourself, who will? It makes it easier to believe in yourself if you've done your homework and tended to your flowers. Allow yourself the capacity to believe in your abilities. Your talents are unique to this world. If you are having a hard time believing in yourself, at least believe in your ability to make this world a better place to live!

"It is never too late to be what you might have been."—*George Elliot*
   Always play fair!

Life isn't fair, but that doesn't mean you have to be unfair. This is why we have rules. Let your mind wander for a few minutes and imagine the game of baseball without any rules. The team with the ball gets to make up the rules as the game goes along. You're at bat, and you hit a ball Babe Ruth would have been proud of. You start to circle the bases but the pitcher stops you and says, "According to my rules, if a batter hits the ball over the fence against my pitching at 6:15 p.m., you're out, and you owe me $100!" I'm sure you wouldn't like that rule change.

If you're in a situation where the rules are fuzzy or there are no rules, what should you do? Should you let your conscience be your guide? That might work if you have a feasible conscience. Better still, "treat others as you would have them treat you." I didn't say playing fair was going to be easy!

13

"Puritanism is the haunting fear that someone, somewhere, may be happy."—*H. L. Mencken*
Always have fun!

Enjoy stuff, all kinds of stuff! We all know life isn't fair but that shouldn't stop you from having fun. Be joyful and let people know you enjoy life. Each of you has come in contact with a sourpuss where each minute you were around them seemed like an hour. Don't *you* be a sourpuss! Enjoy each aspect of your existence! Look at a flower and wonder at its beauty. Be someone you'd be proud of. Be the person your kids can enjoy being around. Enjoy being you who are! Don't let others spoil your enjoyment of life. If you are joyful, you automatically are able to bring fun, joy and a zest for living into the lives of others. Become a beacon for others. Go forth into the world, enjoy yourself and others and have some fun!

"Walk right in, sit right down, daddy let your mind roll on."—*The Roof Top Singers*
You can always put your feet under my table!

This is an old farm saying. It means you are respected and considered worthwhile. People like being around you. If you are a charitable person, play fair and have fun. Your feet will be welcomed under many a table.

"We live very close together. So, our prime purpose in this life is to help others. And if you can't help them at least don't hurt them."—*The Dalai Lama*
Always set expectations!

Always set expectations for yourself, not others. I know each of you has seen mothers or fathers push their kids into activities just because the parents are trying to relive their dreams through their offspring. When the children fail, the parents act as if the world will end. They look upon themselves as failures and that's not fair to their children. Guide and help them, but let them set their own expectations.

"What we have here is failure to communicate."—A line from the movie "Cool Hand Luke"
Never ask questions if you don't want to know the answers!

This is one of my favorites. Aristotle once said that the longer you can get someone to talk, the better the chance that the truth will eventually come out. The truth will come out even when the person talking is trying to hide the truth.

How many of you have been in a relationship where your partner was cheating on you? In your heart you knew the truth, but you didn't ask the question. Was it because you already knew the answer and were afraid of the awful truth? Most of the time when emotions are involved the truth doesn't count.

When was the last time you heard a parent complaining that their son or daughter wasn't being treated fairly by their baseball, softball, football or soccer coach? Never mind that their offspring wasn't good enough. Or is it because their son or daughter wasn't living up to the parent's expectations? Most of the time the question is never asked. Do yourself a favor and start asking questions. More important, listen to the answers, even if it hurts.

"We are all pilgrims on the same journey—but some pilgrims have better road maps."—Nelson DeMille
Life is what happens when no one is looking!

15

Actually someone is looking, and that someone is you. Could you, 20 years ago, imagine yourself as you are today? You are actually where you need to be at this exact point in time. You have to be where you are in order to get to where you need to be later. If that last statement makes any sense, then you have a very strange mind indeed.

Each of us comes into this world with a certain agenda—a beginning point and an ending point. How we arrive at that ending point is entirely up to us. We can take the high road, the low road, the middle road, the straight road, the curvy road, the road less traveled or go through the disease and insect-infested jungle. Whatever road we take is the road we have decided to take. The primary problem the majority of us have is that we have no earthly idea where we are headed. Therefore, any road we travel will do. It takes most of us a lifetime to figure out why we're here, let alone what road we should be on. The road you are on also determines how long your journey will be. Are you supposed to take a 1,000-mile trip on a straight and level road, or a 100-mile trip on a very hilly and curvy road with many washed out bridges along the way? Do you drive 75 mph no matter the road condition, or 50 mph even with perfect road conditions?

There will come a time, after you look at your life's road map, when you will see an exit ramp. Just looking at your road map is a major breakthrough when you are on the road of life. You will probably stop and ponder your decision about exiting the road you are currently on and trying a new one. You might even drive past a few exits and wonder if you should try that one. Is the new road the same as the current one, or is it truly different? Are there more curves, or is it straighter? Is it hilly, or is it more level? What is the speed limit? No matter the speed limit, you will probably drive much slower than the posted limit until you get the lay of the new road. This is new territory.

16

You want to be a cautious driver for the first few miles on this untraveled road. Now, do you really think this new road will get you to your final destination faster and safer than the road you were on previously? Decisions, decisions! Isn't life grand?

Aren't you glad God gave us the free will to try different roads? Aren't you glad God gave us the opportunity to drive at our own speed?

If the current road you are on is too dangerous for you, then you should consider using an exit ramp. Exploring new territories can be fun, but there is always the possibility of getting lost and losing your way. But, if you have your road map in front of you, with your final destination circled in red, it could be great fun. But make sure you don't hurt your passengers when you are driving on the road of life. A life's passenger wants to get to their final destination the same as you.

"Learn to ask good questions and listen carefully."—*Henry Grunwald*
    If you see a turtle on top of a pole, it didn't get there by itself!

Okay, let's be honest. Just how many of you have seen a turtle on top of a pole? None of you? Well, that makes two of us. If you did see a pole-top turtle, what would you think? Somebody must have put it there. No self respecting turtle would climb a pole without a parachute! Have you ever found a turtle shell in a really weird location, and wondered how the turtle got there in the first place? How do you think a turtle would happen to get trapped between the rails of a railroad track, for example.

As a college student, I worked the Norfolk and Western Railroad section gang during the summer. For those who don't know the function of a section gang, they maintain the railroad tracks. They lay track, repair track and replace railroad ties. It's back-breaking work! I can still, to this day, swing one mean sledge hammer. Anyway, I noticed quite a

17

few turtle shells between the railroad tracks. Finally, one day I asked one of the old timers about the shells. His answer was brief and to the point, "They couldn't get out once they got in and died a horrible, hungry death!" So, naturally, I asked how they got in. His answer once again was to the point, "How the heck should I know? I'm not a turtle." I let the reply pass. After all, I was only a 21-year-old college student. And what the heck did I know?

But there is an answer for everything, even for a pole-sitting turtle. His answer really was, "I don't know." Probably a second part to the "I don't know" answer is "and I really don't care." How many times has someone told you he or she doesn't know? I'm sure it numbers in the thousands. I'm equally sure you either believed them or didn't ask what they meant by the "I don't know" remark.

Kids are really good at the "I don't know" response. All right, I agree there are a few things we really don't know. Those things will vary by each individual. I won't attempt to answer the "I don't knows" for you, but for me. How do computers work? I thought I had the answer to that one figured out. However, when I took the computer case off, I didn't find any third-world midgets in there working for 20 cents per hour. I really "don't know" how computers work. And I "don't know" why traffic cops only pick on me! They should be out doing their jobs and catching real crooks!

You get the gist of the "I don't know" syndrome. About 96.3 percent of the time the "I don't knowers" really do know the answers. They just don't want to take the time to try to understand themselves! So, do your loved ones a favor and ask questions when you get an "I don't know." But be careful! That always means that you will have to be honest and insightful with yourself. That is much more difficult and demanding. As Socrates said centuries ago, "You have to know yourself." I wish Socrates hadn't said that. I would rather have been given the credit!

18

Simple Is As Simple Does

"Humor is just another defense against the universe."—*Mel Brooks*
Never let the truth get in the way of a good story!

This doesn't mean that it's OK to lie. What it's really saying, however, is to make yourself interesting. There is nothing wrong with telling a good story. This reminds me of a good story—a confession story.

About 20 years ago, I was visiting one of my best friends, Saul, a Catholic priest. At some point during my visit, Saul showed me his new answering machine. It was one of the first ones with remote capabilities. You can get answering machines today with the same functions for about 50 dollars, but Saul paid about $300 or $400 for that state-of-the-art machine.

I asked Saul how the machine worked and, of course, he wouldn't tell me. He knew that as soon as I was alone with the answering machine, I'd put the world's worst message on it. Saul didn't think a Catholic church's answering machine should have a message telling the caller what the local house of ill repute's hours of operation were. He was probably right!

About 3 weeks later my sister eloped and, of course, she wanted everyone to meet her new husband once they had returned from their honeymoon. We all met at Saul's place, the parish house. Saul was showing Rhett, the new husband, the rectory. I was in the study near the answering machine, sitting in a high-back chair, working on my fourth scotch and soda. It was 2 p.m., after all. Saul brought Rhett into the study but didn't see me sitting in the high-back chair. Saul explained to Rhett, in great detail, how the answering machine worked. He was really proud of that machine! I listened to every

19

word. If Saul could use five words instead of one to explain some-thing, he would instead use ten words. You should have heard some of his sermons. I think he used the words he did just to confuse the little old ladies.

Saul wanted to show Rhett a picture he had on his desk. The high-back chair was facing his desk. Saul approached the desk, found the picture and finally saw me smiling at him. When he asked how long I had been there, I replied, "Long enough to know how the answering machine works."

For once Saul didn't use a lot of words, his one word response was, "S—-!" All three of us had a laugh and went off for another scotch and soda.

At 3 p.m. Saul had to leave the rectory to hear confessions and his last words to me as he left were, "Please don't put anything on the answering machine." I smiled and poured myself another scotch and soda. As I was trying to decide what creative message I should put on the machine, I realized I had not been to confession for about 7 years. In lieu of the appalling message, I went to confession. Saul didn't know I was coming.

I waited in the confessional line for about 30 minutes before I finally got to Saul's confessional to reconcile my sins with God's rep-resentative on Earth. There must have been six or seven little old ladies behind me patiently waiting their turn to tell God what lustful thoughts they've had for the past week. Saul told me confession wasn't nearly as much fun as it used to be. The sexual revolution and the 1960s put a stop to fun confessions.

I finally made it into the confessional and Saul and I go through the whole confession bit. It was hard trying to remember 7 years' worth of sins! I did make up some really good sins for Saul's amuse-

20

ment. Finally Saul asked me, "Is there anything else, my son?" I started to say no, but instead, I snapped my fingers and said, "I have a really good friend who recently purchased a new answering machine and I put the world's worst message on it. What should I do?" There was then about 10 seconds of silence and Saul, God's spokesman, said, "Doug, you s— of a b———." I had just been called a S.O.B. by God's right-hand man.

Needless to say, all we did for the next 5 minutes was giggle. No matter what Saul or I said, we giggled. Saul even forgot to give me penance. When I finally left the very thin-walled confessional, the looks the little old ladies gave me would have made hell freeze over! I've gotten a lot of mileage from this story over the past 20 plus years!

"To be honest with you Samson, it would look much better short!"—Delilah

Don't believe anyone who begins a statement with, "To be honest with you ...!"

If Delilah didn't say this, she should have! Does this mean someone wasn't being honest with you before? Maybe so. I was at a used car lot thinking about buying a car when a salesman decided to start helping me. During the course of the sales pitch, if he used the term "To be honest with you," once, he used it 19 times. I know it was 19 times because I counted. He wasn't being honest with me, and he didn't care what I wanted. He just wanted to sell me that particular car so he could collect his commission check. To be honest with you, (do you like the way I got the cliché in?) I don't believe the salesman knew he was even using it. I know he didn't realize how upsetting that particular phrase is. If there is a moral to this, it's to stop using, "To be honest with you!"

21

"The buck stops here."—*Harry S. Truman*

Always drink upstream from a buffalo herd!

Can you imagine roller skating in a buffalo herd like Roger Miller did, let alone drinking downstream from one? But people actually do that time after time. Not literally, of course, but symbolically. They know they've had problems with buffalo herds in the past, and they swear they will never go near a buffalo again.

But that buffalo herd will show up again and again, and guess what? They go downstream and take a sip of that used buffalo water. It's a mystery! Do yourself a favor, remember your promise to yourself, and stay away from your personal buffalo herd. That way you won't get a bad taste in your mouth!

"To obtain maximum attention it's hard to beat a good, big mistake."—*David H. Hewitt*

Never eat yellow snow!

Unless you are an absolute innocent, this cliché needs no explanation! This one is almost as bad as, "too dumb to come in out of the rain." You know, I actually did meet a guy who was too dumb to come in out of the rain. I was a college student and I needed a summer job. That job ended with me being an orderly in a mental hospital. In those far away days in the mid-60s, the mental institutions were not what they are now. Today, only the very highly disturbed are incarcerated. In the distant past, all classes of mentally disturbed people were locked up.

Some of the inmates I met were really quite humorous. And some were really nuts. At least one was both humorous and nuts! He was also the one that was too dumb to come in out of the rain! Every time

22

it rained he would do his best to get outside and lie down on the grass. It had to be grass. He refused to lie down on anything other than grass. Asphalt or concrete just wouldn't do. I guess it had something to do with his karma. He would lie down, face up, with his mouth wide open. The first time I saw him do it he almost drowned. One of the guards just happened to look outside and saw him lying face up, mouth wide open, choking. Nobody, including himself, was able to explain his actions.

Did I mention that he also thought he was Jesus Christ? One day, while taking a walk on the hospital grounds, he met another inmate walking in the opposite direction. They stopped and introduced themselves. They both professed to be Jesus Christ! What a predicament. After a heated 15-minute debate, the "rainman" relented to the other Jesus Christ. The "rainman" then pronounced himself to be Richard Daley, the mayor of Chicago. After I heard this, I asked him to get me a job as an alderman in Chicago. He really wasn't a very good Richard Daley, since he wasn't able to get me a job as an alderman. He was a much better Jesus Christ, however, because at least he could save me.

Before I leave this thought, there was another very interesting inmate who was about 24 years old. After I knew him for about 2 months, I asked him why he was there. His response was, "I tried to burn down the Pike County courthouse."

"Why?" I asked.

"Well, my wife was screwing around and I couldn't get a divorce because I'm Catholic, so I got drunk one night and tried to burn down the courthouse." Again, I asked why, and he said "Because the marriage certificate was recorded there!"

It made perfect sense to me. You can see that people really do eat yellow snow! Why do we do that?

23

"Slow down, simiplify and be kind."—*Naomi Judd*

Never change a tire on a train!

This doesn't mean that you should never attempt an impossible job. It means sometimes the job is just too big for you to handle by yourself. If it is too big, get help! Can you imagine trying to change a tire on a train? I know a train doesn't have a tire, but tire reads better than iron wheel. If you had the help of a train jack (a train jack is a very large car jack), and experienced people to help, the job would become doable. Too often we try to do big jobs without the proper equipment or personnel.

Remember the first time you ever tried to do something by yourself? The more complicated the task was, such as assembling a child's swingset, the greater chance you had to really mess it up! I hope others were tolerant of your mess ups. I also hope you weren't too hard on yourself. Some examples of this are: the first time you tried to cut up a chicken (I still can't, but I'm a lot better than the first time); paint the dining room wall; write a paper; fill out your income tax forms; cook a dinner; mow the grass; set the clock on your VCR (mine still blinks after 15 years); or have a conversation with the opposite sex. Do you see what I'm trying to say? Too often we set ourselves up to fail. This can happen in anything we do, such as starting a business, a new job or relationships.

Let's say you are having problems with your car. What should you do after you have exhausted all your knowledge? If you are like most people, then your knowledge about cars is very limited. You should take your car to a mechanic. They have more knowledge, equipment and experience than the average person to fix the problem. As for trying to paint your house, I'm sure you asked the sales clerk for guidance

24

in selecting the correct paint brush, paint and other tools needed to start and finish the project.

If you are having problems with a relationship, have you asked for help? If you're like most people, you haven't. That's a mistake. Do you think the problem will correct itself? I've heard these statements time and time again: "I don't want to sound like a fool," or "I can handle it myself," or "it's too personal to discuss" or "things will work themselves out." If you ask for help in other things, why not ask for it in solving relationship problems? Ask for help! But don't limit yourself to just one source. When you get insurance quotes, do you get just one? Of course not! The same thing is true in solving relationship problems.

Whenever the relationship is with a spouse, children, parents, friends or job related, ask for help. When we are talking about emotions, it's most times difficult to see the forest because the trees are in the way. Ask for guidance! It can't hurt. It might even help.

"They do not love that do not show their love."—*Shakespeare*
Charity always begins at home!

Nothing was ever more true. I looked up the definition of charity in about six dictionaries, and none of them have exactly the same definitions of the word. They mentioned brotherly love, God's love for mankind, an act of goodwill, an institution and giving to others in need. But in all six dictionaries there was one common definition, which was that most people would not think of if asked to define the word. That common definition of charity is, "tolerance and leniency in judging others." If we all would accept this simple definition of charity, our relationships would increase in happiness 100-fold.

25

Relationships include all kinds: husband-wife, parents-children, friends, business associates and even strangers. The list can be endless. I'm not saying that you shouldn't judge—you should. We judge every day. But show more than just a little kindness and leniency when you do it.

Don't judge just to make yourself feel better. That shows a weakness in your own character. If you have to put another person down in order for you to feel worthwhile, then you have a great deal of soul searching and character improvement to do. That soul searching needs to start now. Remember, we are discussing charity, and if you expect others to be charitable to you, then you must be someone who can be charitable.

Too often we impose a harsher judgment on our loved ones than what is warranted. In other words, the judgment doesn't fit the crime. I'm not talking about an actual crime, I'm talking about what happens in our interpersonal relationships.

Let's use a very simple example. Your son or daughter is out for the evening and the curfew is midnight. For some reason, your child arrives at 10 minutes past midnight. What do you do? I know of a father who grounded his son for 2 weeks for this minor infraction. Was that charitable? Probably not, if the kid was only a few minutes late. That parent wouldn't listen to any of his son's excuses. The boy could have had car trouble or the movie could have run later than expected. But if he was late because he was trying to sober up, then the 2 weeks of punishment probably wasn't harsh enough.

Quality relationships do require charity. One really good way to achieve that is through communication. Keep the lines of communication open. How does that happen? By listening to what is being said and not adding your two cents worth.

Fear makes cowards of us all! If you are a charitable person, then

26

it will be easy for your children to talk to you because they won't be afraid. Being charitable really does make for quality relationships!

"For every action, there is an equal and opposite reaction."—*Sir Isaac Newton*
   Opposites attract!

There have been studies about this phenomenon and they have borne out what everyone thought. Opposites do tend to attract each other. There has never been a follow-up study to see if the attraction lasts. But if neither party tries to change or fix the other, then the initial fire of attraction should last and improve. What will happen when you don't know and understand yourself and after the initial fires of your overactive hormones have subsided, is that reality will set in. What you found so stimulating in the beginning, you might find irritating later. But, if you never stop your spiritual quest, then the initial fires should never go out. They will only burn longer and brighter!
   If opposites really do attract, does this mean a non-butthead should find a butthead? I don't think so! It would be easier if there weren't any buttheads in this world. Then we wouldn't have to try and change or fix someone. A better idea would be for non-buttheads of the world to unite! Go forth and multiply!

"A cliché is only something well said in the first place."—*Bill Granger*
   Fatigue makes cowards of us all!

Truly a profound statement! Don't make any major life decisions on too little rest. What looks bleakest at 2:30 a.m. might not look as bad at 8:00 a.m. Fatigue can play games with your mind. Before you

27

do decide on anything important, get a good night's rest.

Another cliché that comes to mind is, "It's always darkest before the dawn." I'm sure they were talking about decision making. Don't let anyone force you into a major decision, especially decisions concerning lawyers, without a good night's rest.

"Louie Louie, oh baby, we gotta go now."—*The Kingsmen*

Things are not always what they seem to be!

Do you know the words to the above song, "Louie, Louie?" Everyone thinks they do, but no one really does.

Let's list some examples from history of other things that were not exactly as they seemed to be: the Trojan horse; Judas; the various treaties the United States government signed with the Indian tribes during the 19th century; and the Moral Majority. My favorite story, however, is one you've never heard. It concerns a friend of mine from college, Moby.

Moby told me about an experience he had in New Orleans while he was in the Merchant Marines. Moby was 8 years older than the rest of us when he started college. He enlisted in the Merchant Marines just after high school, because he wanted an education college couldn't provide. He had some very worldly stories to tell. One time, while he was in the port of "The Big Easy," he went to a sleazy bar to drink and, hopefully, get lucky. As luck would have it, he picked up, according to Moby, one fine-looking, tall and buxom redhead. They really hit it off. They drank, laughed, danced and told stories to each other. While they were dancing, Moby decided it was time to make a move. The fine-looking redhead was wearing a very low-cut dress and no bra! Moby said, "She had a couple of great attributes." After a few

28

minutes in sensory heaven, they retired to a back booth with very dim lighting. Just about anything you could imagine went on inside the sometimes friendly confines of this very seedy bar.

Moby and his lady friend were in a back booth, groping each other under the dim lighting. Moby related, "She was one great kisser!" He very slowly slid his hand up her dress, taking his time on his upward journey to joy and happiness. But much to his amazement, what he found at his journey's end was not what he was hoping for! Moby's gorgeous redhead was a man! Needless to say, he was not the least bit enthralled with his discovery. He promptly lost his excitement, immediately left the joint and hurriedly went to a drug store and bought a very large bottle of Listerine.

Everyone Moby was telling his story to was rolling in the aisles with laughter. After the laughter subsided, I asked Moby if he had any inkling that his dazzling redheaded lady friend was in reality a dazzling redheaded man. Moby's reply was, "Well, she did have a very deep voice for a woman. That did seem odd. But, I wasn't planning to sleep with her voice."

Moby's story taught me a few things. First of all, I decided that I, as a 20-year-old college sophomore, would always check the "South Pole" first and save the "North Pole" for later. Second, your first impressions are not always correct. Last, sometimes things just don't go the way they're planned through no fault of your own. Moby's story was a great learning experience, and in his retelling of the story, he was able to help me with my learning. I will admit it did take me a few years to understand that most things are out of my control. If you try to control uncontrollable events, you will never be able to control yourself.

29

The Simple Truth Is

"Blessed is the man who finds wisdom, the man who gains understanding."—*Proverbs*

When someone is buying, keep your money off the table!

This really holds true when you are at a fine restaurant. It especially holds true when you are in the presence of a person with special knowledge.

Grandparents are special people. They have seen more changes than any other generation in history. Learn from them. You can learn from them, but only if you take the time to listen. Without listening, learning will not happen. I'm not telling you to do exactly what they suggest, but take their wisdom and use it in your life. It just might help.

Another bit of advice is, when someone is buying keep your mouth shut. Simply say, "Thanks." How you use what they have to offer is up to you.

I'm reminded of a story my grandfather told me. It seems he was on the front porch swing one night whittling (see cliché, "Always Whittle Away"). A young man, driving much too fast on a gravel road in front of my grandparent's farmhouse, spotted grandpa. He slammed on his brakes, backed up and yelled at Grandpa from the driver's side window, "Is this the way to the Wilson's place?" My grandpa replied, "Yes, it is, but ..." The young man didn't wait for the rest of Grandpa's answer. He put the car in first gear and roared off, throwing gravel behind him. Grandpa just chuckled and waited. The young man came back in about 30 minutes and asked Grandpa if he had a tractor, and could he borrow it? The young man's car was stuck. It seems Grandpa was trying to tell the

30

young man about the one lane bridge being washed out from a big rain the previous night. The young man was in too big of a hurry to wait for the advice Grandpa was trying to give him. The young man finally did ask Grandpa, after his car was pulled out of the creek, "Why didn't you tell me about the bridge being washed out?" Grandpa's reply was, "I tried."

"When we seek to discover the best in others, we somehow bring out the best in ourselves."—*William Arthur Ward*

Don't know your ass from a hole in the ground!

I've heard this phrase from the time I was a young boy. I always thought it meant someone was really ignorant about a certain subject, and that's really what it means. But think about it for a minute. Everyone is ignorant about something. There is no way I could ever be a brain surgeon. And most doctors could never be humble (just a joke to all you doctors out there). Accept people for who they are. Don't judge them by your standards. Judge them for who they are, no more, no less.

"All he needed was a hug."—*Ziggy*

Never put your hand between a dog and its bowl!

The opposite of this is, never bite the hand that feeds you. You know, it depends on the kind of relationship you have with your dog! If you are a caring and nurturing individual, then the dog won't mind if you take its bowl away. It knows you will put that bowl back. You will, won't you?

31

"Life is at its best when it's shaken and stirred."—*F. Paul Facult*

A big dog weighs a ton!

The greater the struggle, the greater the pain, and the greater the chance for personal growth and character development.

"When you are traveling on the road of life, speed bumps are good—they help you miss the potholes."—*Douglas McLaughlin*

No pain, no gain!

This is a cliché that is normally attributed to sports. Take it a step or two further. Use it to refer to the growth you can achieve emotionally and spiritually when you experience the pain of life.

In sports, if you go the extra mile, you will gain strength. That extra strength could give you an advantage over your opponents. Athletes make the pain they have endured in practice count when they are involved in athletic competition, such as basketball.

Remember, we were put here to grow, learn and teach. Whenever pain is encountered, the lessons learned will stay with you forever. You often see youngsters shooting baskets or playing basketball all day and night. Practice makes perfect! The youngsters make their pain count. The reason they endure the pain is obvious. They are striving to become better basketball players. You should do no less.

Everything happens for a reason. There is no such thing as coincidence. You might never know the reason an event happened, but you do have the responsibility to learn and grow from it. Your ability to learn and grow is directly related to the amount of pain endured. Therefore, make your pain count. Don't wallow in self misery. Use your pain to achieve the spiritual growth you deserve. If you've ever

32

hit your thumb with a hammer, you soon learn how to use a hammer to avoid broken thumbs. You learned from your pain and made it count. During your life's journey, you will encounter emotional and spiritual pain. Learn and grow from it. Make it a positive growing and learning experience. The pain you endured will help you and others on the spiritual quest that is life.

"Oh, how I hate to get up in the morning."—*Song by Irving Berlin*
Never trust a day that begins with getting up in the morning!

How do you like this one? This really isn't a negative saying. What it's really saying is, you can never be sure of what will happen today. Let's use a couple of different examples. How many people have started their day with the thought, "I think I will have a fender-bender today," or "I think that Publishers Clearing House will come to my house today with a check for a zillion dollars?" Just start each day with as much enthusiasm and positive thinking that you can. It really does help to trust and believe in yourself. If you don't, who will?

"I have a dream."—*Martin Luther King*
"Every day is a fresh opportunity to continue the quest toward our mission!"

The above is a quote from Harold McAlindon, an early leader in the Boy Scouts. You don't have to be or have been a Boy Scout to take this quote to heart. Our quest is toward continued knowledge.
You can achieve knowledge through many different avenues, but the knowledge gained through self-awareness is knowledge you will keep forever. Self-awareness makes any mission in life attainable. If your

33

mission is world peace, population control or world equality, then good luck because you'll need it. But if your mission is tolerance of others, charity toward others or an understanding that you are important, then each day will bring fresh opportunities and new individuals to us. This will allow us to continue on our mission statement.

Very few of us can have missions that will affect millions of people. But equally, each of us can have an effect on a few people. Who knows, maybe what we did or said today can affect future generations. We all have read that it takes three generations to bring about change. What we do today might have a profound effect on the future. It's worth thinking about and worth doing. Therefore, you have another mission in life. Go out there and spread goodness. It will be repaid 1,000 fold. You will see the benefits of your goodwill in another life. You just won't remember that you started it. Be assured, however, you did help start the process.

"Beauty is only skin deep, but ugly goes all the way to the bone."—*Unknown*
Cute as a bug's ear!

I've heard and used this expression for years. I think it came from my grandfather. But I still don't have the slightest idea of what it means. Since most of us have never seen a bug's ear, they must be cute. You can use it with anyone you love, no matter the condition of their ears. Use the expression with a smile and a hug. It works!

"No day in which you learn something is a complete loss."—*David Eddings*
Always whittle away!

For all of you city dwellers out there, this is an old—very old—farm saying. In the evening the men folk would sit outside, and to pass the time they would whittle. It didn't make any difference if they made anything; they would just whittle.

My grandparents were farm people. Their home was without indoor plumbing or electricity. Neither of them ever learned how to drive a car. If they had to go to town for any reason, they went by horse—bareback most of the time. Town was, in reality, a village of about 150 people with a general store and nothing else. Grandpa was about 80 when he died, and I regret that I wasn't old enough to remember and understand enough of his memories.

Grandpa was a whittler, and one moonlit night in early summer he and I were outside talking and whittling. The talking consisted mainly of Grandpa telling me how the youth of the day were worthless and how they didn't understand work ethic. This was either 1952 or 1953. Grandpa believed the younger generation was "going to hell in a hand basket." I do believe we hear that same thing today! I'll bet my great-grandfather said the same thing. Oh well! I do remember asking my grandfather what he was whittling, and his answer was, "Nothin'." I then asked him to teach me how to do "nothin'." He even allowed me to use his pocket knife. He cautioned, "Don't let Grandma see you usin' it!"

I don't remember any of the instructions about the fine art of whittling except Grandpa was very insistent about whittling away. Too bad I didn't listen to him and understand what he was really telling me. If you insist on whittling toward yourself, you are going to get a nasty cut at some point. You know there is that possibility even before you start to whittle, so why do it? Each of us has whittled the wrong way and cut ourselves. I guess we have to experience some pain before we understand. If there is a moral to this story, it's to use only little knives to whittle.

35

36

Pack Just Enough Baggage For A Simple Trip

"And now these three remain: faith, hope, and love. But the greatest of these is love."—First Corinthians
Love conquers all!

Can love really conquer all? It depends. There are many different kinds of love: love between husband and wife; love between a parent and a child; love between kindred spirits; love between close friends; and love for material possessions. But for our discussion, let's forget about all except the love between the members of a family, a husband and wife and later, parents and children. This cliché is telling us that love will overcome all obstacles. That is true as far as God's love for mankind is concerned. But it's only mankind's love we are discussing here.

For those of us who have children, and that is the huge majority of us, you damn well better love your kids! Our children are our future and our hope. It's our destiny to love our children. I'm convinced if we would love our children, and our children know of our love for them, 98 percent of the social problems we now have would be solved overnight. Teenage pregnancy, juvenile crime and illiteracy would almost disappear. Everyone wants to feel needed and have a sense of worth. Love within a family does that for children. Without love, children turn to other avenues for their sense of worth. Listen, love your children, let them know it and tell them daily. It's easy to love your kids.

Now let's go to a slightly more difficult task, the love between a man and a woman, or in our ever more accepting society, between two adults. Being the romantic I am, I do believe love can conquer all! But you have

38

to choose correctly for love to have a chance to conquer all. Let's think of two imaginary people, Ken and Barbi. Ken is a conservative Baptist. Barbi is Jewish. Ken thinks the Beatles are the best musicians since Mozart. Barbi's favorite is Willie Nelson. Ken's ideal place is the sand and the sea. Barbi breaks out in a rash just thinking about the sun. Ken's idea of a clean house is no dirty underwear in the living room. Barbi goes ballistic if the toilet seat isn't down. Ken is a lawyer in private practice, while Barbi does hair. Ken loves sex, especially outdoors. Barbi really loves sex but, indoors only. Ken wants five kids for his own basketball team. Barbi, on the other hand, thinks one child might be one too many. Both Ken and Barbi find each other very attractive and sultry.

What are their chances of harmony and bliss over the long haul? Do you think there are too many differences between them? Once again, it depends on how much they are willing to work on understanding the other person. Are they willing to work on understanding themselves? Are they willing to work on not judging the other by their own standards? If they can come to mutual agreements on the issues that separate them, of course they have a chance! If they both can go into the relationship with their eyes wide open without trying to change or fix the other, then yes, love can conquer all. Remember, love is forgiving and without judgment. Personally, I don't think Ken and Barbi have a chance. After all, Ken is a lawyer.

"The best things in life aren't things."—*Art Buchwald*
Don't be an jerk!

We are here to offer support, love, a shoulder to cry on, a friendly ear and a caring attitude. Another cliché I'm reminded of is, "Life is a bitch and then you die!" This is a very negative approach toward life, and life has enough unpleasantness without you adding more to it. Try a little kindness!

39

There is an abundance of jerks in this world. Don't add to their population. You know it's much harder to be a nice person, day in and day out, than it is to be a donkey's back side. No one wants to be labeled as or act like a jerk. Then why do we do jerky things?

Why don't you take the road less traveled. Hey, that would be a great title for a book, wouldn't it? Don't take the easy route. Be the person your grandchildren, great-grandchildren, and great-great-grandchildren can tell stories about. Those stories should be about your gratitude and kindness, not about your jerkiness. Just remember: memories about jerks don't bring smiles. They bring head shakes and comments like, "I can't believe anyone would say that" or "she did what?" Your memory should bring smiles. Each of us will be a memory someday. Make sure yours will bring a favorable recollection.

What you should really be concerned with is, if you are a jerk in this life, you are going to have to repeat the life process until you get it right. I talked to a guy who went through past life regression who, according to him, is still paying the price for his really asinine ways from a past life he spent as a pirate in the 16th century. He said he has spent every lifetime since attempting to atone for the pain and suffering he inflicted on others during his pirate days. Why take the chance?

Now, repeat after me, "I will not be a jerk anymore, I will not be a jerk anymore, I will not be a jerk anymore." Do this as many times as you think necessary for the process to take effect. One more thing, sign on the dotted line below stating you have given up your jerkish ways and then date it. Put this copy where you can get your hands on it if you should ever start to revert.

Signature   Date

"Never assume the obvious is true."—*William Safire*

It's the thought that counts, but how much money you spent has a direct correlation to how much thought you put into it!

I'm reminded of the time my 10-year-old son needed a new pair of jeans, so I bought him a pair of Tuff Skins jeans. I gave them to him, he tried them on and they fit! Instead of saying, "Thanks," he took them off, looked at the label and told me he didn't want them. I asked him, "Why?" His answer was, "They aren't 501s." I replied, "What are 501s?"

"Dad, don't you know anything? 501s are the best jeans in the world. All my friends are wearing them. The kids at school will make fun of me if I wore these raggedy jeans! I want 501s!" Being the nice and easy father that I am, I told him I'd exchange the raggedy jeans for the best jeans in the world.

I took them back to the store to exchange them for 501s. I was astonished to discover that the 501s were more than twice the price of the Tuff Skins! I told the sales clerk that I wasn't about to take out a second mortgage for a pair of jeans. Needless to say, I didn't leave with the 501s.

I returned home and told my son about the price difference. Once again, I handed him the Tuff Skins. He looked at me with quivering lips and very moist blue eyes and said, "Dad, the kids will laugh at me!" I couldn't have kids laughing at my son, but I wasn't about to pay double for a pair of jeans. I was on the "horns of a dilemma." What to do?

I suddenly remembered I thought I had a pair of 501s. I checked my closet and guess what? I did! I did what any parsimonious father would have done. I removed the label from the new pair of Tuff Skins and replaced it with the label from my old pair of 501s. It took me more than 2 hours to accomplish my deceitful task. It was a much harder project than I originally imagined. I soon found out why they were called Tuff Skins.

I completed my deception and gave the jeans to my son the next day before school. The first thing he did was look at the label, smile, gave me a hug and said, "Thanks, Dad!" He wore his new jeans to school that same day.

When I returned home from work that evening, I asked him if any of the kids at school noticed his new jeans. His humorous reply was, "Yeah, they wanted to know where you bought them. I think they thought they were neat!"

I tried the same thing with my car. I installed a Lexus insignia on my Ford. It didn't work!

"Often the best way to win is to forget to keep score."—*Marianne Espinosa Murphy*
Don't use satire as a weapon!

Satire is a sign of weakness. Comedian Don Rickles uses satire as the main theme in his comedy routine, and he's funny. The reason he is so successful is that most people like to see others squirm and be uncomfortable. Almost everybody knows his comedy routine, and they take the satire as comedy. His routine gives the audience a reason to laugh at others' expense. In real life, however, the same doesn't hold true.

Nobody likes to be made fun of. Satire is an easy way to hurt someone without being held accountable for your comments. You can say, "But it was only in fun," or "Can't you take a joke?" That is total bull. Most of the time, the use of satire in a relationship is used only for control and hurt. Satire is easy. It's another way to say you are somewhat less than I am. Satire puts others on the defensive.

I recently read an article in the *Catholic Digest* stating satire is a

product of pride and self-righteousness. Satire is one-upmanship. There is no place for it in any committed relationship. There is no place for it in any relationship—period. When someone gives you an opportunity for a great zinger, don't use it if it will hurt another's feelings. The only thing satire can bring to a relationship is a dividing of the people involved. People don't like to be reminded of their shortcomings or made fun of. Don't further enhance their shortcomings. You are there for support, love and nurturing. Don't mess it up. For God's sake, don't let the truth get in the way of being a loving person.

"Character consists of what you do on the third or fourth tries."—*James A. Michener*
Don't fall on your sword!

I'm reminded of cowboy movies I've seen, where a cowboy will shoot himself in the foot because of his carelessness. Anytime you carry a loaded weapon, you always have that chance of shooting your foot.

We live in a much more complex world than any cowboy could imagine. Therefore, we have many more swords to fall on. What we have to do is limit those swords. There is no way we can eliminate them, but if we know about the swords, then we have an advantage. The advantage is simple. We understand the pitfalls, and we understand the damage a sword can do.

"Don't tug on Superman's cape. Don't spit in the wind. Don't draw against that old Lone Ranger, and you don't mess around with Jim."—*Jim Croce*
Don't draw against the Lone Ranger!

43

What happened every time a bad guy drew against the Lone Ranger? That old Lone Ranger would shoot the gun out of the bad guy's hand. He would then deposit the bad guy in the local jail. In the final scene, the Lone Ranger and Tonto would gallop away into the sunset on their trusty steeds, Silver and Scout. After the Lone Ranger rode away, the bad guy would always get out of jail by bribing the sheriff. But that's another story.

"This is the worst trip I've ever been on."—*The Beach Boys*
The wagon always rolls fastest at the bottom of the hill!

At the top of the hill, the wagon is completely at rest. It hasn't started its downward descent yet. All it takes is a nudge to get it started. How large and heavy the wagon is will determine how big a push it will take to get it started. The total weight of the wagon is determined by how much of a load it's carrying plus the weight of the wagon itself. Sometimes it will only take a small push and other times it will take a mighty shove. It might even take more than one person to get it started, and it might even take more than one shove.

The wagon's journey downhill starts very slowly. If you tried to stop the wagon at the top of the hill, it would not take too much effort as it has not begun to pick up much speed. If you decide to stop it halfway downhill, however, after it has picked up more speed and momentum, it would take a supreme effort to slow its progress. You could try to throw out some extra weight. Even then it will probably still take two people using the hand brake. If you wait until the wagon is near the bottom of the hill, after it has gained its top speed, you are too late. The wagon will reach its own final destination no matter how much you want to stop it. The wagon's course and fate have already been set. Only the wagon's speed and weight will determine where it will finally stop.

As you can see, once the wagon starts rolling downhill, it gets progressively harder to stop the speed and momentum it picks up. It will be harder still if you haven't lightened the load the wagon is carrying. If you don't try to stop the wagon, it will eventually crash.

Relationships are a lot like wagons. First of all, don't put excessive baggage on the wagon. The lighter the load the wagon is carrying, the easier it will be for you to stop the wagon after someone has given it a nudge. If both parties are working together at stopping the wagon, then you have a chance to stop its fatal rush downhill. Good luck.

"Show me the money."—*A line from the movie, "Jerry Maquire"*
It's not the money that's important, it's the principle!

Does this mean that most lawsuits are over principle? If the above cliché is correct, then what about the little old lady who sued McDonald's for megabucks and won because she spilled a cup of hot coffee on her lap? Would she have been just as pleased and happy if the jury would have denied the lawsuit provided McDonald's would only serve lukewarm coffee? After all, her principle was upheld. Yeah, right.

"Build what, in the middle of a desert?"—*Noah*
Never let your elephant mouth override your hummingbird arse!

Think before you talk! This reminds me of another story about elephants and hummingbirds.

An acquaintance of mine, Dan, told me a story about being an elephant. Friends of his had invited him for dinner to celebrate his 40th birthday. Before the dinner started, Dan was informed that another guest whom he didn't know was also invited to dinner. The other guest

45

was a high school and college friend of the host. Dan was asked to please not tell gay jokes as the other guest was gay. Dan was also informed the other guest, besides being gay, was also a lawyer. Dan had a joke for every occasion, and he promised his hosts he would refrain from any gay jokes. His friends told him that lawyer jokes were still fair game, however. I guess that means even lawyers think lawyers are full of it.

The guest arrived. Before dinner drinks were served, dinner commenced and wine was served, and after dinner drinks were served. After the dinner table was cleared, Dan poured himself another drink and started talking to the gay lawyer. Dan can't talk to anyone for more than 5 minutes without telling a joke, and tell a joke he did. It was an ethnic joke that involved the Jewish race. The body of the joke isn't important, but the punch line was, "You would think they were a bunch of Jews, wouldn't you?" The response from the gay lawyer was, "No, they're not—but I am!"

Dan said his response was, "Oh." (See, when you are up to your ears in shit, it's best to keep your mouth shut!) The gay lawyer left within 10 minutes.

Dan told me from that day he has not told another joke that involves race, religion, ethnic origin or sexual content. Dan hasn't been telling many jokes since he made that oath to himself.

You see, Dan is not an offensive individual, and he meant no harm. But he did offend and harm another. Remember, other people have convictions, and those beliefs might be different from yours. If they are, don't try to force them to accept your beliefs as gospel. But, if you do feel the urge to offend someone, offend yourself. Don't offend a loved one. Better still, don't offend anyone. Start practicing today on strangers, and it will carry over to your loved ones. You owe this to your loved ones. You also owe it to yourself.

46

Love Is So Simple

"Today I found no sorrow."—*Creedence Clearwater Revival*

It's not what you have been through that counts, it's what you will be through!

Into everyone's life, a little rain must fall. Sometimes it's a light mist and sometimes it's a massive cloud burst. Your moral character will determine how you will fare after the storm. Will you respond as though it were a sprinkle or a raging thunderstorm? Everyone can tell you what you have been through. No one can tell you what future experiences you will encounter. Whatever those experiences might be, use them to learn and grow spiritually. Your spirituality determines how you will deal with adversity. Adversity determines how you will develop spiritually. Sounds like spiritually and adversity are tied together, doesn't it?

I can think of no greater adversity than the death of a child. How would you respond if you lost your child in a tragic accident? Would you blame yourself? Would you seek revenge? Would it ruin your life?

A few years ago, a 20-year-old girl was murdered during a camping trip in one of the Western states. The murderer was eventually apprehended, charged, convicted and executed. We read about this kind of tragedy in the newspapers every day. What made this terrible murder extraordinary was the response of the murdered girl's parents.

After their initial feelings of shock, disbelief and anger, they wanted revenge! Justice would soon be theirs! The killer of their little girl was to be executed. Then, something miraculous happened. Their hearts began to soften. They knew the execution would not bring their beloved daughter back to them. The grieving parents even

47

started a correspondence with the killer! This correspondence was both written and by personal visits. The parents even asked the court, in person, to commute the death sentence to life imprisonment! Talk about compassion!

These people actually believed in forgiveness! The parents were already highly developed spiritually before their daughter's murder. The terrible tragedy didn't change their spiritual beliefs, but only made them stronger. I pray to God I never find out if I have that much compassion.

"Live so that when your children think of fairness and integrity, they think of you."—*H. Jackson Brown*
Always be a role model for your kids!

Raising quality children is the best thing we can do in our lives. Rearing children is a lot easier if you have the same qualities you are teaching your kids. Do the things necessary for your kids to want to use you for an example; therefore you must parent by example. Remember, our children are our greatest asset. Ask yourself if you are doing anything you would not want your children doing. Play fair and show compassion.

"It's man's mission to learn to understand."—*Vannevar Bush*
Always remember it takes more than water for flowers to grow!

48

Growth is the optimum word in this little ditty. We need to grow to become the people we need to be. Flowers need water to flourish. They also need good soil and plenty of sunshine to grow into pretty flowers. So do we as spiritual beings need more than just the basics to nurture and develop into higher spiritual beings?

I'm sure you all understand the analogy about flowers needing more than water to grow. Let's take it a step further and see how we can get the flowers of our souls to grow and flourish. What do we need besides water to develop? More important, what can we offer to others besides water to help them grow? First, what do we need to help us grow to our potential? We know we need to be non-judgmental, charitable, trusting, fair and to have a zest and enjoyment for life. They are really ours for the taking. All we have to do is believe we have those attributes. Oh yes, then we have to practice, practice, practice. You don't become proficient in anything with-out a lot of practice. The same holds true when we become spiritual beings. Once we've started the transformation in ourselves, we can offer to help others with their own transformation. That offer, to help others, need not be made on a conscious level. Others will see what we have become and will wonder why we are different. We are now helping others learn by example. Sounds pretty simple, doesn't it? You know, it actually is.

Once you make the decision to do more than just nourish your soul, things will start happening to you. You will start to enjoy life and others around you will start to enjoy you. Do good things for yourself and become a person with compassion. Give yourself more than water and wondrous events will start to take place. Don't get discouraged. It will happen. Build it and they will come. Hey, that sounds like a line from a movie!

"Everybody makes mistakes, that's why erasers were invented."—*Unknown*
The trouble with doing something right the first time is nobody appreciates how difficult it was to do right!

I guess this is why we all have to make mistakes in life. I just love reading about an "overnight sensation." Margaret Mitchell was an overnight sensation with her first and only novel, "Gone With The Wind." Never mind that it took her more than 10 years of research, long hours and countless revisions before it was finally published. After all that, she certainly did get it right the first time! I wonder how many erasers she went through?

"Our greatest glory is not in never falling, but in rising every time we fall."—*Washington Irving*

The trouble with doing something right the first time is, there is nothing to do later!

If we always do it right the first time, how would we ever learn? One thing we all have in common is that we learn by our failures. Failures are what we do before we get it right! At times it seems as if we will never get it right and are doomed to have failure after failure. Let's take a look at some of our failures.

When we were young, we accepted failure as a part of growing up. Think back to your first bike riding experience. It was probably very painful. I know mine was. I can still remember getting on my bike at the top of a small hill which overlooked a baseball diamond. The bike's brakes didn't work and, of course, I couldn't steer. I wonder if my parents gave me that no-brake bike on purpose? The baseball bleachers were on the same side of the hill I was coasting down. Since I couldn't steer or stop, the bleachers made for a very effective and painful brake. The pain did decrease the learning curve. Eventually, I became a skilled bike rider. I still had a few mishaps, but they were few and far between.

The same is true when we start any new experience. We make mistakes, have failures, grow and learn.

Remember when you were learning to play a musical instrument? My instrument was the trombone. After 6 months of practice, I came

50

home and played "Twinkle, Twinkle, Little Star" for my parents. After I finished my solo, my parents said, "That was nice son. What was it?" I couldn't carry a tune in a bushel basket as a 10-year-old and I still can't as a 50-year-old. There will be some things in your life that you'll never be proficient at even though you practice long and hard. When we're young, we're willing to experience failure after failure because life is new. Experience is how we learn, and we are expected to fail.

Let's move forward a few years to adulthood. Once again, think about our failures. Do we experience failure because of new experiences? Or, is it because we are unconsciously setting ourselves up for repeated failures? Are we putting ourselves into positions that the only possible outcome can be failure?

There is another saying we have all heard, "History repeats itself." Individuals also repeat themselves. We all know failure hurts. Repeated failure hurts even more because we start seeing ourselves as losers in the game of life. The only real failure in life is not attempting life. I can't think of any endeavor where failure is not a possibility. But be careful with repeated failures. I've known people who say they have 20 years of experience. What they actually have is one year of experience 20 times!

It really galls me when someone who is not competing or has never competed classifies someone else as a loser when they fail. Just think of all the Super Bowl losers. They aren't thought of as coming in second to the best team in the world. The sports writers and the general public look upon them as losers. That's a crock! How about Olympians? Once again, if they don't bring home the gold, they are looked upon as a little less than whole even though they have competed against the best athletes in the world.

The same is true of us in our everyday pursuits. We are judged by

51

society's standards, not by our own. There is absolutely nothing wrong with failure as long as you learn from it. If you don't learn from your failures, you are destined to repeat them over and over again. You might even have to repeat this life over again. For some of you that would really be fun; but for the majority of us, it could be very painful. So, get out there and learn! At least try to learn your lessons by the second or third lifetime!

"It's one thing to learn about the past, but it's another to wallow in it."—*Kenneth Auchincloss*

If you live with one foot in the past and one in the future, you can't help but mess up today!

This is a very true statement. Let's break it down into its simplest parts with a story.

Let's say that 17 years ago you interviewed for a great job with a great future. You interviewed for the position of director of product development. The position commanded a starting salary of $100,000 plus an annual bonus. You even had an inside track for the job, as you were dating the personnel director. The interview went wonderful. You answered all the questions correctly, the interviewer liked you and you knew the company's history and its goals. You would have even liked the job. During the course of the interview, however, the refried beans you had for dinner the night before started to have an effect on your gastro-intestinal system. You fought and fought the digestion process, but after fighting for more than 2 hours—it was a really long interview—you lost the battle! The sound effects were incredible, as was the smell. You did what any sane person would do; you acted as if it didn't happen. But you weren't able to pull it off.

You found out later you were the most qualified candidate for

52

the job, and the interviewer would have liked to hire you. But the large corporation didn't offer you the position. Oh yeah, the personnel director you were dating broke up with you soon after. After the fiasco, you finally did land a job with another, albeit much smaller, company at a salary less than 40 percent of the larger company's starting salary. You are still with that same small company today. Your present salary still hasn't matched the starting salary of the larger company, and you feel as if your talents are being wasted in your current position. You haven't had an original idea in 16 years!

From time to time, you check on the progress of the person the large corporation hired instead of you. You see his steady and slow advancement, and you can see what the future will hold for him: more of the same steady and slow advancement. I should mention the personnel director eventually married the person the large corporation hired instead of you. They have three beautiful children plus a vacation home in the mountains.

Whenever you have a few drinks and you talk about the job you lost, the envy in your voice becomes apparent. You talk about what might have been. Self-pity is not very attractive. To this day you haven't touched another plate of refried beans.

I know this story is far-fetched, and it probably has never happened. But, the point of the story is there. You can't change the past, and you can't worry about what might have been for your future. Use your past to help you in future decisions. But, live your life in the present. By doing so, you are not burdened by past mistakes nor are you troubled about future ones. One word of caution, however: know what your mission is and above all, know yourself.

53

"Success is always temporary. When all is said and done, the only thing you'll have left is your character."—*Vince Gill*

Never argue with the guy who has the mike!

If you've ever been to a comedy club, I'm sure you witnessed a comedian being heckled from an audience member. I'm also sure the comedian won in the war of wits with the heckler. Why is that? Well, I can think of two reasons.

First, the comedian has the training from countless hours of being heckled in other clubs by every conceivable dumbhead in the world. Second, and probably most important, he has the mike. There is no way the heckler is going to get the last word, but oh, do they try!

Now, a second question pops up. Why does the heckler keep trying? Does he really think he's funny? Is he trying to gain control of the room? Or does he just like to hear himself talk? No matter the reason, the comedian will always have the last word. Remember, he has the mike and the control. How many times have you seen someone try to take the mike away from someone else? The guy with the mike has the power; the guy without it doesn't. So why would anyone try to do battle when one person has all of the power?

I'm very thankful that there have been people who have spoken up to the person with the mike. Let me give you a few examples of just that: England standing alone against Germany in 1940; the women's suffrage movement in the early 1900s; the American Revolution; Truman's victory over Dewey in the 1948 presidential race; the Vietnam anti-war movement; the 1969 New York Mets; the 1969 New York Jets; the 1980 U.S. Olympic hockey team; Jackie Robinson; Ghandi; the English fleet against the Spanish Armada; Upton Sinclair's exposé on the meat packing industry at the turn of the 20th century; and Rachael Carson's book, "Silent Spring," dealing with the dangers of DDT.

Others who have tried to stand up against the person with the mike and lost are: the various Indian tribes against the onslaught of the whites; John Brown; the Confederate states of America; Ireland vs. England; the Hebrews at Masada; Spartacus; William Wallace; Thomas Beckett; the Tucker automobile company; Joan of Arc; and probably the one voice that has had the greatest impact on the world—Jesus Christ!

But, if you do decide to argue with the guy with the mike, remember—be prepared to lose. The world loves rooting for the underdog. But if the underdog loses—and it happens more often than not—the world will also say, "I told you so." Pick your crusades well. You have to be willing to lose all; you can't hold back. Don't say, "I'll try." Instead say, "I'll succeed." This holds true in everything you do, whether it be in school, business, hobbies, causes and especially relationships.

"Life is the test of us."—*Corrine Roosevelt Robinson*

Always remember that life is difficult, though our culture tries to deny it at all costs!

Life is tough, and it has always been tough. Why is our culture trying to tell us otherwise? For many reasons we have been led to believe life should be easy. This message is being portrayed to us constantly, primarily through the television media. According to television, all you have to do in order to get the person of your dreams, at least for one night anyhow, is drink the Silver Bullet, drive the right car, use the correct spray deodorant, dress with designer clothes and wear Nikes. It's that simple.

55

Now we all know that television isn't real life. But at some level of our consciousness, we've believed television to be the truth. I can remember watching "Father Knows Best" and asking my mother why she didn't wear high heels when she cooked and cleaned. I asked this question one evening when she was doing the dishes. She stopped washing the dishes and walked out of the kitchen, without saying a word. She returned in a few minutes wearing a pair of high heels. She went back to the kitchen sink, picked up the dish rag, walked over to the kitchen table and sat down. She still hadn't said a word. After a few more minutes of silence, she motioned for me to come to her. I walked toward my mother and as I got within arms length, she put her arms out, put her arms around me and gave me a big love hug. That hug must have lasted a full 2 minutes. Mom then gave me a kiss on the cheek and handed me the dish rag. With a big smile she said, "Look son, I have on high heels, you finish the dishes." I never asked my mother about high heels again.

Denying life's difficulties is something of a recent phenomenon starting after World War II. For 30 years after the war, the United States was the world's industrial giant. It was the only country in the world left intact. Things were easy for us and we became complacent. We expected things to always be easy. We were told life was not hard, and that was a lie.

We have to realize that life is hard and will continue to be hard. That can be a blessing. Without struggling we don't grow, and as we all know, growth is paramount. Most of us need to struggle in order to grow.

Think of all the great accomplishments in history. All had a great deal of difficulties and hardships. For example, the Revolutionary War, the War Between The States, The Great Depression and the Western movement involved many people who experienced life at its hardest.

56

Think of some of the personal challenges you've faced. Were they easy? No, they were tough! Going through a divorce, a death or the current trend in business downsizing are stumbling blocks that will test a person's character. Be glad for the difficulties you've survived. If you make it through, you have a chance to grow and develop great character because of your personal challenges. You will learn things about yourself you didn't think possible before you began your personal struggles. Great pain can and will afford great growth.

There is another saying that the only thing in life you can count on is death and taxes. Well, there is another thing you can count on: life is hard. Earth is the universe's great laboratory for personal growth. What we learn here, in this time, will benefit us the next time we come around. Each of us is here to learn, and that level of learning is different for each person. Without learning from our struggles, we would have to repeat our difficulties and pain all over again. I know very well that I don't want to repeat this life's pains again. I want a new adventure. I want to learn more. I want to graduate to different struggles next time.

Although life is hard, and will continue to be hard, take joy in your struggles. Don't believe television. Be glad you are growing and learning. Don't waste your pain. Make pain into a positive instead of a negative. Make it count. Don't think things will ever be easy. Take pride in your personal triumphs.

"Tomorrow, tomorrow, it's only a day away."—*Little Orphan Annie*
Don't do today what you can do the day after tomorrow!

If you look up the definition of a procrastinator in the dictionary, my name, address and picture would be listed. This is a really neat cliché to use at a party. It will get a chuckle.

57

Everyone knows a friend, relative or neighbor that habitually puts things off. I can think of a couple of reasons why people procrastinate. One, they don't like to do a particular task, such as mowing the lawn, cleaning the house, writing letters or visiting their mother-in-law. They simply put the dreaded responsibility out of their mind. That way, they are able to postpone the hated task for an indefinite period of time.

I had a friend who was forever starting a project but never finishing it. He had the ability to finish his projects, but he simply got bored. His strength was the planning and initial starting of a project. His house was one unfinished project after another.

One summer day he decided it was time to paint the exterior of his house. He bought the paint, brushes and drop cloths to start and finish his project. When he was about halfway through the painting, in mid-August, he went inside to get a glass of water and noticed how drab the living room wall was. He and his wife had been talking about remodeling the living room for the past 3 or 4 years. He decided August was the right time to start the remodeling project. He immediately went to the basement and returned with a sledge hammer. He destroyed that living room wall in a matter of minutes.

The living room stayed in major disarray for more than 2 years! The house never did get painted during that same time. However, other projects did get started. He started a deck, started a kitchen remodel and bought an old car to restore. Needless to say, nothing ever got finished on time.

You are probably asking yourself how his wife was able to put up with his many unfinished projects? A better question might be, "Are they still together?" The last I heard, they were happily married for more than 20 years. Once, I did ask the wife about his many unfinished projects and why it didn't seem to bother her. Her response was,

58

"I knew what he was like when I married him."

She accepted him for what he was. She was willing to accept the entire person just the way he was, faults and all. Eventually, all the projects were finished. But new projects were always in the planning. Their life together was never boring.

59

Pure and Simple

"But oh! The things I learned from her when sorrow walked with me."—*Robert Browning Hamilton*

If you are going to play with the big dogs, you have to pee in the big bushes!

This reminds me of a story a guy named Herman told me. It seems he had some very beautiful bushes in his front yard. He worked very diligently at the trimming, weeding and watering of his bushes. He was intensely proud of those bushes. According to Herman, they were the best bushes in the entire Western world. But then fate stepped in, in the guise of a German Shepherd. That German Shepherd really didn't care just how much effort Herman had put into the care and maintenance of those fantastic, award-winning bushes. It seemed every time the dog walked by Herman's house, he would stop and do what all dogs do—take a pee on the bushes. The dog had to establish his territory, and the bushes were part of it.

Herman wasn't impressed with the German Shepherd's ability to pee on his bushes. Whenever he saw the dog stop by, he would yell, throw things and generally curse the dog. But nothing Herman did would detour the dog from its appointed rounds, and his bushes were dying from repeated dog dousings.

After a few months of observation, Herman did observe a pattern in the German Shepherd's routine. Herman was always home every other Saturday morning, and he noticed the dog would trot by around 10 a.m. He had a brain storm. (Let me add at this juncture that Herman was not a dog lover nor was he a particularly nice man.) His idea consisted of getting a flat 2x2 piece of steel. He attached two electrical wires to that piece of steel. He then connected those wires to

60

a 220-volt circuit breaker located in his basement. He placed the piece of steel directly under the dog's favorite bush. His ambush was ready! He could see his bushes from the concealment of his basement window. Now all he had to do was wait for the dog to show up on Saturday. The day arrived and that poor German Shepherd appeared at 10 a.m. exactly. The dog stopped at his favorite dying bush to once again establish his territory.

Herman was at his assigned post in the basement, lying in wait for his victim, just like a snake. He waited until the soon-to-be-sterile dog finished his sniffing and raised his right leg. At the moment the dousing started, Herman struck! The dog got the full effect of the 220-volts! He jumped about 3 feet straight up, yelped and took off down the street howling in great pain. Herman said, "I never saw that mangy cur again!" The dog was only doing what came naturally, "just minding his own business." Still, the dog got hurt, possibly mortally. At the least, he will never be a father.

You are probably thinking the moral to this story is about just how cruel and vicious Herman is and how he should spend eternity in everlasting hell. First, I don't believe in hell. Second, Herman was only doing what he thought he had to do to defend his property. No matter what the rest of us think about his actions, he thought they were justified. The real moral is that sometimes really nasty things can happen to us through no fault of our own. That's just the way life is.

Each of us has known someone who has had truly terrible things happen to them that they didn't deserve. Some of them have survived the ordeal and others haven't. You have also known people who have had infinitesimal mishaps in the road of life. You'd think they had lost everything because of the way they carried on.

Two stories come to mind about how people handled difficulties

61

during their journey on the road of life. One is the "Gloria story" and the other is the "Jackie story." First, the Jackie story.

Jackie never had to do without. She was born with a silver spoon in her mouth. She went to the right schools and she married the right man. Life for Jackie was one of wealth and opulence. She believed that a hardship was only having a three-car, instead of a four-car, garage.

Jackie's upstairs bathroom had developed an unnoticed drip that leaked into a downstairs closet. Two days before hosting a large dinner party she discovered the water damage. She immediately called various restoration companies for emergency repairs to the closet. None of the dozen or so companies she called could respond in 24 hours like she wanted. Needless to say, she was greatly irritated! She knew her dinner party was going to be a total disaster because of the damage to her closet. Jackie went on in great detail about the way she was treated by the restoration companies. After all, didn't they know who she was? She was still re-telling the great pain and anguish she received at the hands of the contractors 6 months after the fact. With each telling she was expecting sympathy. She couldn't comprehend why the listeners didn't understand her pain.

Now the Gloria story. Gloria was born in a very poor family in the South. She was severely abused during her youth, both physically and verbally. Gloria literally watched her father kill her mother before her very eyes when she was about 11. Gloria became pregnant at the age of 14 and was put into a home for unwed mothers. After the pregnancy, she entered a job corp program. There, one of her male counselors took her under his wing and convinced her to work the streets for him, becoming a prostitute. She worked the streets until she was about 19. Of course, she always turned the money over to her counselor/pimp. On more than one occasion she was physically afraid for her life. Gloria always knew she had to get out. All she needed was the courage! With only the clothes on her back, she caught a bus to Kansas City, Missouri, in the middle of the night.

After being in Kansas City for a few years, she applied at the local Ford plant and became the first black woman to work in an automobile manufacturing facility in Kansas City. Gloria told me that the first few years of working at the plant were almost as hard as working the streets, and leaving on that bus. She survived the Ford plant, just as she survived the streets. She is now leading a very productive life!

A lot of bad things happened to Gloria during her childhood, things which she had no control over. It seemed when things couldn't get any worse, they did. She had the will and determination to rise above her situation. Her past could have destroyed her, but she didn't allow the past to stop her future. No one can say that it was easy for her. It wasn't! However, Gloria was able to put the past into its proper place—the past.

When something bad happens to you—and it will—don't blame God. Just work through the terrible times. If you allow it, the difficult times will give you greater character than you ever thought possible. Growth through pain is everlasting. I'm not advising you to purposely bring pain into your life. However, when pain does occur, make it count! And for heaven's sake, don't sweat the small stuff!

"I can't get no satisfaction."—*The Rolling Stones*
    Always remember a woman's or a man's first name when making love!

This is just a really good idea.

63

"I don't need a road map. I can find it myself!"—*Moses*

The grass is always greener on the other side!

Of course your neighbor's grass is greener! You're looking at your neighbor's grass from the distance of your lawn. What you can't see is the crabgrass, nutgrass, dandelions and mole runs. Most of us are in search of something. It could be happiness, perfection, money, or a meaningful existence. When we see what others have that we wish we had, we become impatient. We want the same, and we want it now! We don't know how our neighbors were able to achieve their green and lush grass or how long it took. We certainly don't know the amount of hard work that went into their lawn. We just know we want it and we want it now! What we really need from our neighbors is the knowledge of how they were able to achieve what we want. We need their road map. Don't just wish for your grass to be as green and weed-free as your neighbor's, you need the right instructions. You don't want to be lost in the desert for 40 years, do you? Do you get my drift?

"Let the sunshine in."—*The Fifth Dimension*

Don't think money can buy happiness!

The only thing money can buy is stuff. Sure, stuff makes life more comfortable, but we all see the same sunsets, oceans, mountains, trees and flowers. A BMW and a Ford will both get us to the same mountains and oceans in the same amount of time. What difference does it make what type of vehicle you have as long as you get to your destination?

Will it really make any difference how much money you make or possessions you acquired 100 years from now? What's important in this lifetime is love between people. If you happen to be blessed with money, good! Don't let it go to your head. Don't think you are a better person because of your material stuff. The only thing money proves is just how lucky you are!

"You talk the talk, but do you walk the walk?"—*A line from the Movie, "Full Metal Jacket"*
    Don't suck hind tit!

This is another old farm saying and you are probably wondering to yourself, "What the devil does this mean?" When a sow (mother pig) would nurse her piglets (offspring), the piglet that ended up nursing at the back teat, more often than not, would get shoved away by its siblings. The little piglet wouldn't get enough to eat, and if that happened enough times, the piglet would die. Life doesn't cut any slack for little piglets. The piglets have to look out for themselves if they expect to survive. Of course, they don't know they will be bacon in a few months anyway. The piglet that is sucking hind tit also has a better chance than the other piglets of being crushed by the sow when she decides to move. The sow doesn't give the little piglet enough time to get out of her way. So you see, the piglet at the end of this particular food chain is fighting not just for food, but also for survival. The same holds true for many of us.

We have elected to suck hind tit when we let people put us down. We let others tell us what to think, what to do, and especially if we expect to keep up with the Jones', what we should spend our money on. We don't get the nourishment we need in order to survive emotionally and grow spiritually in this world. If you continue staying at the hind tit, you will only get more of the same. We need to take control and responsibility of our lives. We have no one to blame other than

65

ourselves if we continue going to the end of the food line. We must take responsibility for our actions in order to control our own destiny.

What is the best way to start taking control? I can only tell you how I stopped sucking hind tit. I started to listen to others more knowledgeable than myself, and I asked numerous questions of those people. If I didn't understand what they were saying, I continued asking more questions. One Christian minister asked me if I was as thick-headed as I appeared to be. I told him I was and continued asking more thick-headed questions. I also read book after book. I started with Christian books and went on to the new-age thinking books, took the Meyers-Briggs personality test, and read books on psychology, U.F.O.'s and life after death. I still even had time to read Stephen King books. I was developing my philosophy. But, there was one thing that was constant during my journey, and that was my desire to listen, ask questions and learn. You must listen in order to learn, and the only way to learn is to listen.

Another constant was other people's genuine belief that their way of thinking—their philosophy—was the right way to think. No, not the right way, the only way! I don't think an individual doctrine is totally right or wrong. Every philosophy has something you can learn and use. Every person you meet has something for you to discover. Some learning you will discard immediately, some you will have to think long and hard about before you discard it, and some you will embrace. At times you will experience great anguish because you will question your long-held beliefs.

Finally, you will have your own philosophy—it might be the belief of your childhood, it might be a brand new one, or it might be a combination of your old and new thinking. The journey will not be easy—nothing worthwhile is ever easy—but it will be exhilarating.

66

You will find out things about yourself you didn't know existed. Always question, because without questions all answers are right. You need to know what is right for you. Whatever the outcome, you are to be congratulated on starting your journey, and it will be one without an ending. Once you start, it will become a life-long journey toward knowledge, the knowledge of self and of becoming. Once you know yourself, even a little bit, you stop being that last little piglet. Today is not too late to start. Every journey starts with that first step of asking the first question.

"You learn in life the only person you can really correct and change is yourself. You can't do that with anyone else."—Katherine Hepburn
  Never lick a flagpole when the temperature is below freezing!

(See cliché, "Never Pee on an Electric Fence") When I was in junior high school, I had a friend who just wouldn't believe his tongue would freeze to a flagpole if he placed it on one when the temperature was below freezing. If he stuck his tongue on a freezing metal flagpole once, he must have done it a dozen times. Sure enough, it stuck every time. More than a few times, he would leave some of his tongue on that freezing flagpole. And his tongue would bleed every time. I'm sure it hurt, but he never did learn. If you see a gray-haired 50-year-old man walking around with a bandage on his tongue, it's probably my friend from junior high school. Say "hi" to him for me.

  There is a moral here. Some people just don't learn, and others won't learn until they get hurt over and over again. You know, I think pain is a way of life for some people. It's their way of getting attention. They have such a low opinion of themselves that pain gives them their

67

identity. Pain without growth is wasted. Make your pain count. This is from the "First Book of Doug," chapter five, verse nine.

"The moon is high and so am I. The stars are out and so will I be, pretty soon."—Roger Miller
It's not even good enough to be called bad!

What's worse than bad? Here are a few words that fit the bill: evil, amoral, terrible, horrible, wicked, vile, sinister, corrupt, repulsive, obscene, contemptible, depraved, wretched, appalling, ghastly and dreadful. How can something be so bad that is not even good enough to be called bad? Here are some examples: the Kansas State football teams of the 1970s; Nixon's attempt to cover up Watergate; the Vietnam War; the price of new cars; the cost of a college education; all lawyers; the Jenny Jones' talk show; self-righteous people; the Missouri football teams of the 1980s; and turnips.

Don't forget to include the car in front of you on an interstate entrance ramp that starts to merge with traffic. You look over your shoulder to see what the oncoming traffic is like and the car in front of you stops in the middle of the exit ramp for no earthly reason. You rear-end her. Guess who gets the ticket—you!

There will be bad things that happen in your life, and you will have to cope with them. But bad things really can build character. Without bad stuff, how will we recognize good stuff when it happens? Because of bad, when good happens we are able to handle it with compassion and humility. After all, shouldn't we always practice compassion even with ourselves? Some bad things will be humorous when we look back on them years later (see cliché "Murphy's Law," whatever can go wrong will go wrong.) Adversity will help you build your character, grow spiritually, learn and hopefully, teach.

68

"He sure did make a wrong mistake."—*Yogi Berra*
    All general statements, including this one, are wrong!

There are always exceptions to any rule. Statements such as, "the kids of today are only interested in themselves;" "all doctors think they are God;" "all lawyers are swine;" "I never watch television;" "1960s music is much better than today's music;" "you think you are always right;" "you never listen to me;" "but you should know what I'm thinking;" "you think more of your job than me;" and "I will never trust anyone ever again."

    General statements have a grain of truth in them, but one grain of sand does not make a sandbox. You have to know the rest of the details. After you know all the details, a general statement will become a specific one. You can work with a specific statement to help correct a problem. General statements can only lead to nothing. They won't help you in your quest for growth, teaching and learning. Find the underlying cause for a general statement and work on it.

"Some people say that there's a woman to blame, but I know, it's my own damn fault."—*Jimmy Buffet*
    It's not my fault!

Each of us has heard small children use this expression. They use it to avoid punishment and reprimand and to place the blame on another. The problem is that too often children grow up and continue to use the same tactic in adulthood.

    Pretend you are quietly reading a book one night and you hear the sound of breaking glass coming from the family room. You immediately dash from your chair to see what's the matter. You find your one and only Waterford crystal vase broken! Your 8-year-old daughter is in

69

the room with the broken vase and a basketball. You take in the scene and ask, "What happened?"

"It's not my fault," your daughter answers. "I just touched the ball with my foot and it bounced up and hit the chair. Then it bounced again and again and again and again. I tried to stop it from bouncing all over the room, but I couldn't. It almost stopped bouncing, but then it took the biggest bounce ever and hit your vase. I didn't do it! It's not my fault!"

Your daughter is doing her best to avoid pain and to place the blame on something else. She knows the basketball can't defend itself. Her rationale won't work, but she is going to try anyhow.

We live in a society that does the same thing. If something is rotten in your life, blame your problems on something else. If you are having trouble at work, blame your boss. If your children are doing terrible at school, blame their teachers. If you are up to your neck in credit card debt, blame the credit card companies. If your marriage is in trouble, blame your spouse. The list is endless. If everything else fails, you can always blame your parents! That's the best one. After all, your parents were raising you during your formative years. Blame your adult problems on them! This reminds me of another story.

Beverly was 38 years old with two children. She had been married twice, with each marriage lasting about 6 years. Her first child was the product of her first marriage, and the second was a product of a one night stand while between her two marriages. She said she gave more than 100 percent of herself to both marriages, but her husbands expected more and more from her. Her teenage sons were having problems in school. Their teachers didn't understand them. Because of all the stress she was under, she decided she had contracted CFS (chronic fatigue syndrome.) She knew she didn't deserve her problems, and that her parents had to be the reason for her adult dilemmas.

70

Beverly decided to change her parents. She asked for and received her birth certificate. Her mother and father were listed as her paternal parents. Beverly didn't stop! Her parents couldn't be her real parents! She knew her blood type, so she told her parents she might need a blood transfusion so asked them what their blood types were. They were both compatible with hers. She had a picture of herself blown up along with a picture of her parents. She then sent the pictures to a lab for comparison. The results weren't conclusive. That gave her hope! She even asked her sister, older than her by 15 years, if she had given birth to an illegitimate child. Her sister hadn't.

Beverly knew her problems were not the result of her actions. Her adult problems had to be because her parents weren't really her parents. Real parents would never allow bad things to happen to their children, even when the child is an adult.

Beverly just wanted someone else to blame for her actions. She should have known her parents were, in truth, really her parents. All three of them had a common trait—dumbness!

71

Simple Simon

Even with our best intentions, things can go wrong through no fault of our own. Allow me to tell you a story about things going wrong.

First, I need to set the stage and the list of characters. I was once a young high school boys' basketball coach living in rural Illinois, with a wife and an infant son of 6 months residing in a house trailer. It was a very mild Tuesday in mid-February when the events started. The basketball team was playing a conference rival in a neighboring town about 50 miles away. Of course, we took the school bus to the game. What a game it was! We led the entire game by as many as ten points and were really playing above our level. We were making unbelievable shots, playing tough defense, making great passes and committing no turnovers. Then came the awful, appalling and dreadful final two minutes of the fourth quarter.

We started missing lay-ups, and we turned the basketball over in the most imaginative ways. With only 6 seconds left in the game, one of my players saw an open man under the basket, and he made an excellent pass to him. The problem was that the open man was one of the officials! The ball caromed off the official into the hands of an opposing player. The opposing player took four dribbles and launched a desperation shot from half court. We lost the game by two points on that halfcourt heave. I was not a happy coach. My team showered and left the non-friendly confines of Pleasant Hill, Illinois.

During the course of the game, the weather changed dramatically, as can happen in the Midwest. The temperature was about 40 degrees

72

when the game started and was in the mid-teens when we departed. Guess what? The heater on the school bus decided to break. It stayed broken the entire 50 miles back to good old Perry, Illinois. The trip back was in cold and total silence.

When we finally arrived home, I thought it would be a good idea to have a team meeting. A morale booster! I gathered the team inside the high school where it was warm. My theme during the meeting was one of encouragement, telling them to forget about the past game. At one point, I used the well worn cliché of, "It's not whether you win or lose that counts, it's how you play the game." The only comment I received was from Greg, the team's philosopher, who asked, "Then why do we keep score?" It got a laugh from his teammates and no response from me. I thought to myself, "That's a heck of a good point!" I ended the meeting and we went home.

I arrived at my humble house trailer and immediately checked the washer/dryer. We had a combination unit. It would wash your clothes, and then you would switch the unit to dry them. What a deal—especially if you were living in a limited space house trailer. The reason I was checking the "machine from hell" was that it had developed a water leak the previous day. I, with my great knowledge of machines, had fixed it, or so I thought! It was a front loader with a round glass door, and the first thing I did was to listen for the tell-tale sound of a drip. I didn't hear one.

I looked through the glass and didn't see any water in the machine, so I opened the door. Did I mention that the outside temperature at this time was 10 below and it was midnight? I opened the front loader's glass door. Guess why I didn't see any water through the glass door? It was because the water level was above the top of the glass. There must have been a million gallons of water in there and it spilled

73

out in a torrent, traveled down the carpeted hallway and ended its journey in the living room. We opened the side door of the house trailer and started sweeping as much of the water outside as possible. After we finished, we used all the towels we had as sponges. After the sponging, we directed three floor fans toward the very wet carpet. We finally went to bed at about 1:30 a.m.

Now it was my infant son's turn. My wife and I made an agreement just the day before that if our son awoke for his early morning feeding before 4 a.m., I'd get up with him. If it was after 4, she would get up. Guess what? My son started screaming at exactly 3:54 a.m. My son was—he still holds the record—the slowest eater on the face of this Earth. He would eat for about 5 minutes, take a 15-minute break, and then start eating again. This went on until 5:30 a.m. I should add that during the feeding, my son had a bowel movement to end all bowel movements and it leaked out. I changed his diaper, changed my clothes, put him in his crib and went back to bed at 6 a.m.

The alarm went off at 7 a.m. Somehow I got up and went to the kitchen to make a pot of coffee. No water! The pipes had frozen during the night! I decided, then and there, to go to school for a much needed shower, a shave and ten cups of coffee. I left the house to go to school. Did I also mention that it snowed about 8 inches during the night? I scraped the snow and ice from the car, all the while thinking about that steaming cup of coffee and a hot shower. I got into the car, put the key in the ignition and turned it—nothing! The battery was dead!

I went back into the trailer and checked the water once more— no water! I called the local garage and requested a jump start. They were there within 10 minutes. That is one of the nice things about a very small town. You can be anywhere in town within 10 minutes and still have 5 minutes to spare. Heavens be praised, the tow truck arrived and got my car started. I let the car warm up for about 15 minutes before I started for school. I backed out of the driveway, but the car didn't seem to be handling right. At first I thought it was the 15 feet of snow I was driving through. I was wrong! I opened the car door, got out and looked at the tires. The left front tire was flat. I immediately drove back into the driveway, called in sick and went to bed. That was a really poopy night. In hindsight, it was only a small inconvenience on the road of life.

Nothing important happened and the effects weren't long-lasting. We fixed everything, shot the washer, played more basketball games and my son eventually grew up to became the fastest eater on Earth. I guess what I'm saying is, "Don't sweat the small stuff!" Let life happen. Always knowing there will be speed bumps in the road of life makes it easier to smile and have fun. You can't control everything!

"There is in all the past nothing to compare with the rapid changes now going on in the civilized world."—Henry George

Never pee on an electric fence!

This is one saying that should not need an explanation, right? Wrong! Let me tell you a story about my son, Corey. When he was about four, he was staying with his grandfather, who was a grain farmer. One night at dusk, they went outside to check his electric fence. You see, he had put in a garden in a small corner of one of his fields. To protect his vegetables against raccoons and rabbits, he enclosed the garden with the fence. My son didn't know what an electric fence was, and he really did pee on it. Needless to say, he had a very shocking story to tell. My 4-year-old son didn't understand electricity, but he certainly learned about it quickly. The lesson stayed with him because it hurt.

75

Most people would never purposely pee on an electric fence. However, I'm sure you know people who have peed on an imaginary electric fence with the knowledge that it was an electric fence. Drug use is a great example of that imaginary electric fence, but that one is too obvious.

How about relationships? It's my way of thinking that relationships are in the realm of the great unexplored, uncharted and unknown territory. Let me delve into the past for just a minute. We, in the latter half of the 20th century, are on the cutting edge of relationship reform.

Let me explain. Before World War II, things were different. Men were men and women were a step or two below. Men ruled the roost. Whatever men said was the rule. They were the bread winners, and the woman's place was in the home. Men went to war, and women raised the kids. Men went into business, and women stayed home and cooked. Men went to the bars, and women drank in private. Husbands had the affairs, and wives looked the other way. Men decided where they would live, and the women picked out the wallpaper. In other words, men controlled the electric fence.

Things are different now. What happened? World War II happened, and women and society changed, never to go back to the old rules. The rules have changed. Things were the same for hundreds of thousands of years. Women can now vote, drive a car, wage war, earn a living, smoke, drink to excess, get ulcers, ask for telephone numbers and get divorced for no reason. What caused this great change? Economics! Money is the great equalizer. The factories during World War II needed manpower to produce the weapons of war, and womanpower went to the factories in mass. And women continued to work. They wanted their economic freedom.

76

We are in a new society, and are just starting to learn and accept the new roles we are playing. In 100 years from now, the sociologists will wonder why we had so many problems when simple logic would have prevailed. However, we are in this time, not 100 years in the future. We have to cope with the realities of today. Because men and women are exploring uncharted territory, there will be many bouts with electric fences. Some will be small, 2-feet-high fences you can step over. Others will be 12-feet-high fences that will take much thought and cooperation to get over. If you must pee on an electric fence, do yourself a favor and turn the power off first.

"When you can't have what you want, it's time to start wanting what you have."—*Kathleen A. Sutton*
  If my aunt had balls, she would be my uncle!

This really seems like a stupid statement, doesn't it? Well, if you are only interpreting it literally, it is. But as you all know by now, that is not how to interpret the clichés in this book. What it's really saying is don't try to be something you're not.

Don't be envious of others. They might have more money, have more material possessions, be better looking, smarter or even have great kids. Even if they have all that, there is still one thing you possess they can never have. That one thing is your character. No matter how hard they try, they can't be you. Each of us is a unique individual with strengths that no one else has.

We have discussed how you shouldn't be a jerk. Let's take it a step further and use our imagination. You are now the richest person on Earth. You have more money than the king of New York. You are also gorgeous! Let's really get carried away; your IQ is 217! Sounds pretty good, right? I'll bet you think that now I'm going to throw in something awful! Something like, this person is going to die at a very early age. Well, I'm not! The lifespan of this particular person will be whatever the average lifespan is—somewhere between 75 to 80. You are probably saying to yourself, "Heavens yes, I'll trade places!" Remember from an earlier saying, the reason we are here is to learn, grow and teach. By learning, growing and teaching we help others along with ourselves to a higher spiritual plateau. We certainly can't do that if we are someone else, now can we?

Each of us is special in our own way, with a unique mission in life. What we have to do no one else can do. I hope your special mission is how not to teach others how not to behave. You know that happens—we learn how not to behave by the examples of others. Each of us has known someone whose character was so bad we would actually pray to God, "Please don't let me be like that person."

Each of us is here for something special, and we can't be special if we are someone else or we wish we were someone else. Envy has no place in our spiritual development. Do the world a favor and be satisfied with who you are. No one can be you better than you. If you work at being you, you can even become a better you than you already are. Boy, was that a mouthful!

"You are my soul and life's inspiration."—*The Righteous Brothers*
Never have superficial relationships!

78

Let's see, how many different kinds of relationships are there? Business, friendship, causal, family, sibling, children, spouse, significant other and many, many more. It's my belief that we are put in this life to learn as much as we can from others. We must learn our lessons well. I, for one, don't want to come back too many more times to this same place simply because I didn't learn my lesson this time around. How can we learn if we don't open ourselves up to learning? We can learn from many avenues: life's successes, life's failures, but especially from others.

Learning starts early. In the beginning we learn from our parents, then from our teachers, friends and religious leaders. We learn from everyone we meet. So if you accept the premise that we are put here to learn, and that profuse learning will come from others, you must accept the fact that you and I are the "others" to everyone else. So, what does this mean to us? Very simply, we must learn and teach. How can we learn what we have to learn? "Becoming aware" is how a good friend of mine put it. If you aren't learning from others, then you are cheating yourself. You definitely are denying others their chance to learn from you.

You are probably asking yourself, "What does learning have to do with never having superficial relationships?" The answer to that question is everything. If you don't let others into your life, how can you be trusted enough to truly learn what is important? If you aren't willing to share your thoughts, beliefs, fears and hopes, how can you expect others to share their inner-most thoughts? If we are to grow, and by growth I mean spiritually as well as intellectually, we must interact with others. We don't have to take their beliefs as gospel, but we must listen with an open mind and heart. Without that, you will never know who your next teacher might be. The lessons we learn will vary from the very simple to the very difficult.

Let me give you an example of a simple lesson. I was once a salesman for a very successful family business which consisted of a father and his three sons. No, not the television series. The father started the business in the late 1950s. His sons came into the business from the

79

mid-1980s to the early 1990s. Each of the sons was in charge of a different aspect of the business. None of them were acquainted with the struggles their father had to go through in order to start and maintain a thriving and very successful business. They didn't know what it was to be without. I'm not sure they even knew how to spell "struggle." There was not one ounce of compassion in their bodies. They were not kind people. The lesson I learned was a very basic one—that life without compassion is like life without chocolate. And we all know that chocolate is one of the four basic food groups, just as compassion is one of the basic tenets of our emotional and spiritual development. I doubt very much that they will ever have compassion for their fellow human beings. Their only chance for growth is to go through some type of trial or struggle that will test their spiritual mettle.

If you can take the chance to open up to others, your life will be rewarded ten-fold. We can learn from everyone we meet, from the clerk at the check-out counter to the CEO of a Fortune 500 company. All we need to do is take the chance and be receptive to the power we all possess. That power is listening. By listerning we learn. And by learning we grow. Especially listen to the ones closest to you: wives, husbands, children, mothers and fathers. Be kind, gentle, compassionate and never enter into superficial relationships.

"The degree that we love will we be loved."—*Ralph Waldo Trine*

The one in control is the one with the least amount to lose!

80

This holds true 98 percent of the time! The person who controls the toilet paper controls the restroom. The one who sets the highway speed limits controls the highways. Your job is controlled by your employer. In all of the above examples, control is set by someone other than yourself.

Think of a few things you have control over. You are in command of your money, your time, hopefully your children and most of the personal decisions you make. When it comes to interpersonal relationships, control is definitely in the hands of the one who really doesn't give a hoot about the relationship. It takes two dedicated people to make a relationship work. If one of the two has decided that the relationship sucks, then control of the relationship is firmly in the hands of the suckee. The poor sucker doesn't have a chance.

There aren't any words of wisdom in this case except for this: Don't let your relationship deteriorate into such a state that one person doesn't care about continuing it.

Relationships are any close encounters with another life form—your spouse, kids, parents, employer or your friends. Since you are the only one you have control over, start being a nice guy. Nice guys of the world, unite. By uniting, we will have done our duty to bring a little joy into this world.

"If you believe in forever, then life is a one-night stand."—*Righteous Brothers*
You have to put the past behind you before you can move on!

Another way to put this is, don't let your past get in the way of your future.

OK, so you were screwed over by a member of the opposite sex, probably a spouse. Does that mean you will never trust another? I certainly hope not!

I've met many people who say they have put a brick wall around themselves so they won't be hurt again. That wall will keep the hurt out. It will also keep your future joy out. In order to have joy, you have to take chances with your heart. Brick walls don't allow your

81

heart to take chances. If you must have a brick wall, put it around the person who hurt you and give others a chance. Don't dwell on the past. The past is where it belongs—in the past. Don't make it a part of your present or your future.

Give others the same chance you would want someone to give you. Hey, I'll bet I could rephrase that last one to read something like, "Do onto others as you would have them do onto you." That almost sounds like an Old Testament saying, doesn't it? If you do have a brick wall up, take it down immediately!

Here is another compelling reason to remove that wall of bricks. Remember, we are here to learn, grow and teach. Do you really want to do this all over again? You don't want to be stuck trying to learn the same thing for the next 1,000 years, do you? Doesn't it make a lot more sense to remove that brick wall obstacle now? Besides, with the bricks up, your opportunity to learn, teach and grow spiritually is practically non-existent. How can you grow inside a brick wall? You can't! Open up your heart and let the sunshine in! Hey, there's another great title for a song. How about that!

"Prayer is less about changing the world than about changing ourselves."—*David J. Wolpe*
Don't pee into the wind!

At one time or another most males on this earth have taken a leak against the wind. The wind blew it right back and they got wet! All of us at some time have taken a pee into the wind, women included.

Taking a leak into the wind is a lot like drawing against the Lone Ranger. The outcome is pre-ordained. No matter how many times we do it, the results will be the same! Yet, many of us continue to pee into the wind over and over again. Why is that?

82

We all have read about how welfare affects generation after generation. Once someone goes on welfare, the chances that their children will also be on welfare is staggering. The same thing is true of children with alcoholic parents. Studies have shown their chances of choosing an alcoholic partner are much higher than the norm. Women who become involved with abusers tend to do so over and over. Why? Is it because they continue to have someone else to blame for their failures? It's a whole lot easier to place the blame on someone else, rather than on themselves. Remember Flip Wilson's famous line, "The Devil made me do it!"

It's very hard to change even little things. Change takes tremendous courage and determination. Change takes time, and patience is something most of us don't have a great abundance of. Once we make the decision to change, we want it to happen, and happen now.

A good friend of mine has a prayer he uses often regarding patience. It goes something like this: "Lord, grant me patience and grant it now."

So why do we pee into the wind? I believe the answer is simply that we don't know any better. We haven't taken the time to know ourselves. If we would really get to know ourselves—I mean really know ourselves—we would not have nearly as many wet pant legs as we do.

"We had joy we had fun."—*The Four Seasons*
Don't get wrapped around the axle, or don't get bent out of shape!

Take things as they come. I guarantee that life will go on, and the world will not stop for you. Life is hard enough without you making it harder by getting bent out of shape.

OK, so your wife forgot to make the house payment this month. Will yelling and screaming accomplish anything? OK, your husband forgot your birthday. Are you going to remember he forgot your birth-

83

day and be incensed every time you think about it for the rest of your life? So your son forgot to take the trash out on trash pickup day, and you lectured him for 30 minutes about responsibility. Is the lecture going to get the trash picked up before the next trash day? Why take our frustrations out on the ones we cherish the most?

Don't take life so seriously. World peace will not be affected by an error or omission a family member makes. So what if you didn't get the raise you were hoping? Yeah, I know you deserved it. But venting your rage on those closest to you will only cost you in the long run. It will probably even cost you in the short term.

If one of your children breaks your favorite family heirloom, shouting won't repair the damage. Nor will telling your offspring what a klutz he is. That cherished treasure can be replaced.

You were not put here to be a tyrant. You're here to grow, learn and teach the fine art of becoming. Start by becoming a kinder and gentler person! Who knows, when you come back to this Earth in a couple hundred years or so, you just might see how kind and gentle our society has become. You can tell people you are the one who helped start the kind and gentle process hundreds of years ago! You would be a legend for all mankind!

"Accept that some days you'll be the pigeon, and some days you're the statue." —*Robert C. Anderson*

When you are up to your ears in shit, it's best to keep your mouth shut!

At one time or another, everyone who has ever lived has been faced with an impossible situation. No matter what you attempted to do, thought about doing, wanted to do or actually did, you only made the situation worse.

Stop for a moment and use your gray matter to think back to a time when you really made a horse's rear end of yourself. You probably felt like you were about 2 inches tall. While you were making the supreme fool of yourself, time stood still. Now ask yourself a second question. Why did it happen? Ninety-nine times out of 100 you insulted someone. Why did you do it? Yes, I know, you didn't do it on purpose. However, the insult was still there and hurtful to another. Did you tell an off-color joke or simply use bad judgment? You certainly shouldn't tell an off-color joke to a group of ministers, but maybe you did. This reminds me of a story about not keeping one's mouth shut.

One of my best friends, Matt, a Catholic priest, was a visitor in my home when one of my neighbors, Grant, came over to meet Matt. Grant is highly opinionated, loud and self-serving. Grant was introduced to Matt, but I neglected to inform him as to Matt's occupation. You know in hindsight, I probably did that on purpose. After the introductions and a few drinks, Grant decided to tell one of the dirtiest jokes imaginable. As Grant's luck would have it, the joke consisted of whips, nuns, dogs and chains. I didn't try to stop him from telling his joke.

Grant was very proud of himself at the telling of his terribly funny joke. Only after the deed was done did I tell him, "Grant, did I mention to you that Matt is a Catholic priest?" Before our very eyes, Grant lost a foot in height, his pallor increased to almost white, and he tried to become one with the chair. I will say this for Grant, he immediately apologized for the joke and excused himself saying, "I have to go walk the dog." His family didn't even own a dog.

Even though Grant didn't think before he engaged his mouth, he did have the sense to cut his losses and escape. The moral of the story is the next time you insult someone, just apologize and make your escape. Staying and trying to defend yourself or your point of view will only make matters worse.

85

Is Simple Enough

"Take this job and shove it."—*Johnnie Paycheck*
It's only a job!

How do you define yourself when you're introduced to someone for the first time? Do you always end the introduction by stating what you do for a living? If you don't tell people what you do for a living, they will probably ask you. Another cliché is, "Do you live to work, or do you work to live?"

A recent newspaper article stated that new college graduates can expect to have nine to 13 career changes during their working years. That's not nine to 13 different jobs, but different careers. That's unbelievable! What you do for a living is not even a close second to who you are. Who you are defines your outlook on life. Your job helps pay the bills—nothing more. Sure, you might be really good at what you do. You might even love your job. You might make a ton of money at what you do. You might be viewed as a leader in your chosen field. You could even write a book about life's simple instructions and become famous! Will your job tuck you in at night? Will it hold your hand when you are sick? Will it jump on your lap and ask you to read it a story? Will it tell you it loves you? Will it share a sunset with you? Will it tell you a humorous story? Will it look into your eyes, ask for nothing and smile?

When people ask me what I do for a living, I have a standard line: "According to my boss, not a heck of a lot!" It always gets a smile—most times a laugh—and often they say their boss thinks the same thing. I never do tell them what I do because it doesn't make any difference. I will be the same person no matter what I do or how

86

much I make. They have to accept me for who I am, not for what I do, or how much I earn.

Now it's time to tell you a story about a party I attended a number of years ago. A good friend of mine, Tim, a lawyer, decided to have a surprise party for his wife. Tim asked if I would be the official picture-taker. I accepted the task. There were probably 150 attendees at the surprise party, mainly lawyers and their spouses. During the course of the evening, I was asked by a group of five or six wives if I was a professional photographer. My response was, "No, I'm just a friend of Tim's." Then they asked what law firm I was with? I told them I wasn't a lawyer, but a lighting designer. They just looked at me and said, "Oh" in unison, turned their backs and walked away. I felt insulted but didn't say anything. I went back to taking pictures. Within 20 minutes another group of wives asked me the exact same questions, but this time I slightly exaggerated my answer when I told them, "I'm a nuclear physicist under contract for the government working on the Zona bomb, and I can't discuss my work with you as it is ultra-top secret. One of you could be a Russian spy!"

This time they didn't turn their backs on me but wanted to know more about me and my work. Again, I told them I couldn't discuss my work, but to ask any other questions they might have. After 15 minutes of very lively conversation, I informed them I had to get back to taking pictures. As I was leaving the group, one of the wives invited me to a party she was having in a few weeks.

I certainly didn't become a nuclear physicist in a few minutes. I was the same dull person as before. My views and beliefs stayed the same. Nothing changed except the lawyers' wives thought I just might be interesting, but only because they thought I was a nuclear physicist. They found out I was interesting, but it wasn't because of my work. I

87

was interesting because I am interesting. I declined the party invitation and never did tell them I wasn't a nuclear physicist. I wonder if I would have been invited to the party if I would have told them I was a sanitary engineer? What do you think?

"Get a job."—Sha-Na-Na

I'm willing to go to work, but I'm having trouble finding the car keys!

How many times have you ever used that excuse? I'm convinced the vast majority of us don't like what we do for a living. There have been many studies done through the years and in each instance the findings were the same. The overwhelming majority of us don't find any satisfaction in our jobs. The most recent findings stated that 70 percent of the American workforce dislikes their jobs. The reasons given ranged from hours worked, wages, their immediate supervisor, boredom and stress. The average worker today as compared to 1963 puts in an additional 160 hours annually with no additional compensation. That is an additional month per year.

So what should we do to make our work interesting? I propose that we must start having fun working. How are we to do that? Well, it would help immensely if each of us would get to know ourselves. Find out what you can do in your job to make yourself more interesting, more knowledgeable, more creative and more fun loving. It'll carry over into other aspects of your life, such as your job. But remember it's truly only a job. Jobs might come and go, but you are constant. You are not more or less because of your job. Be enthusiastic about life. Go out there, laugh and have some fun!

88

"Don't let your love go away."—*The Four Seasons*

Don't bite the hand that feeds you!

Everyone has heard and probably used this saying at least once. I'm sure your parents have used this one on you about your first job, visiting relatives and certainly chores. Why don't we, however, take it a step further and use it in connection with our everyday lives, particularly our relationships?

Why would anyone try to hurt another person, especially one who is very dear to us? The only reason I can think of is—I can't think of a reason! Our relationships give us substance. It makes life worth living. It gives meaning to life. Relationships help us to grow, learn and teach.

This doesn't mean you can't have arguments, disagreements or even heated debates. But, it also means you should never consciously bring harm, disrespect or belittlement to any of your loved ones. Your job will not tuck you in at night. Nor will it comfort you in time of need. Only people can, especially loved ones. The people who will stand with you during times of stress are your loved ones. If someone reaches out to you for help, don't turn your back on them. Don't bite that hand. You will need it someday!

"Come on people now, smile on your brother. Everybody get together, try to love one another right now."—*The Young Bloods*

What goes around comes around!

I know this is one saying every one of us has heard at least 1,000 times. It has its origins in the Bible. Take your pick from the following: Ecclesiastics 11:1, Proverbs 19:17, Matthew 10:42, Second Corinthians 9:8, Hebrews 6:7, or my personal favorite, Galatians 6:9: "Let us not

89

become weary in doing good, for at the proper time we will reap a harvest if we do not give up." I especially like the thought that by doing good I will reap a harvest of everlasting peace and charity. I also hope there is a lot of humor in the afterlife. God has to have a really weird sense of humor, considering all the stuff he puts us through. Just joking God. There is no way I would want to get God p.o.'ed at me. Life is hard enough without that kind of misery. Remember what God did to Lot's wife. With God's help, she started the Morton Salt Company.

Since we are products of enlightened scientific thought, how about Newton's principle, "For every action there is an equal and opposite reaction." Or, how about this Bible verse, "Sow and so shall ye reap." Or, how about these 20th century sayings, "Do onto others before they do upon you," or "Win at all costs."

This gets us back to the original thought, what goes around comes around. I guess it depends where you are at your own stage of spiritual and character development on how you will answer these philosophic questions. If you are in the early stages of character development, then you will want the "come around" to happen immediately. If you've developed and progressed into the later stages of spiritual evolution, then time and space become meaningless.

If you believe another has wronged you and justice will come to them, if not in this life at least in the afterlife, you still have work to do on your character. It's your character you are concerned with. It's your character you can work with. It's you that you can change. It's you that you can do something about. It's you who can "come around." Most important, it's you who you have control over. So if you want something pleasant to come around, forget about what others say and be concerned with your development. Forgive and forget; your spirit will thank you in this life and for many lives to come.

90

"When you need someone to count on, count me in."—*Gary Lewis and the Playboys*
Trust is the ability to believe in another in spite of their screw-ups!

Let's go back to the "do nots" and add a few more sayings you are never to use under any circumstances. Don't say the following: "I told you so;" "If only you would have listened to me;" "I told you it wouldn't work;" "You didn't do what I said, did you?;" "Why do you always screw up?;" "I'll have to fix it for you;" "If I told you once, I've told you a thousand times;" "Why can't you be more like (fill in the blank) _____?;" "You did what?;" and "You aren't very smart, are you?" I'm sure you can think of a few more to add to this list of trust-breakers.

Yeah, that's right—trust breaking. The more you are positive about another's ineptitude, the more inept they will become, and the more they will grow to resent you. The quickest way to sever a relationship is to always be right—no matter what. The ability to trust another means you have to live with their screw-ups. At some time your loved ones will screw-up. Everyone screws up—even you! Don't make your loved ones feel any worse by using a cutting remark!

I'm reminded of the time my former spouse removed the road tar off our new car with steel wool. She wanted to surprise me, and she did! She said later she couldn't remember if you were supposed to use steel wool or not. The car did have a unique paint design after that! That was a definite screw-up.

We include our loved ones into our lives on purpose. We should have enough faith in our good judgment to allow them the same chance we would give ourselves. After all, they are extensions of us. We do trust ourselves, don't we?

91

"Contrary to what many think, listening is an intensely active—not passive—process."—*Dr. Scott M. Peck*

If a frog had wings he wouldn't bump his behind on the rocks!

I'm sure you can think of many "ifs" that you've used in your lifetime. "If only I had listened." "If only that cop hadn't been there." "If only I had listened." "If I hadn't had that last beer." "If only I had listened." "If only I invested in Microsoft during the first offering." "If only I had listened." "If only I hadn't invested in silver when it was $50 an ounce." "If only I had listened."

If a frog had wings, they wouldn't be in those great Budweiser commercials. Budweiser would probably have had to use ducks instead, and it just wouldn't be the same! I just can't imagine three ducks talking like Donald Duck saying "Bud-weis-er," can you?

"Country music is three cords and the truth."—*Harlan Howard*

There is no such thing as a free lunch!

How many people do you know actually believe that the world owes them a living? As a bonafide Baby Boomer, I was led to believe that there were certain things I could expect. More specifically, they were my birthright! Among them was a happy life, a boatload of money, two exceptional kids, a lot of fun and a loving spouse. There was to be only one spouse, two cars, vacations every year, one job in my working life (at the most two jobs) and it was to provide us with a really good retirement. Oh yeah, all of this was to happen without a great deal of worry or trouble. So what happened? As Forrest Gump was running across America for the second or third time, a spectator ran with him for a short while and watched as Forrest stepped in some dog poop. He

92

immediately said, "Man, you just stepped in a big pile of shit!" Forest replied, "It happens!" Shit really does happen. Maybe we can find out why it does occur, and when it does occur, what we can do to lessen its impact.

"To improve is to change. To be perfect is to change often."—*Winston Churchill*
   Birds of a feather flock together!

If you really want to change your ways, change the flock you're flying with. If you want to be a born-again Christian, start going to church. If you want to stop drinking, go to Alcoholics Anonymous. If you want to make a lot of money, work 16 hours a day and start your own business. If you want to be loved, start loving. If you want to express yourself, write a book. If you want to be a jerk, go to law school. If you don't like your situation in life, change your environment. It's that simple. But, it will be the hardest thing you ever do!

"History must repeat itself because we pay such little attention to it the first time."—*Blackie Sherrod*
   First time a victim, second time a volunteer!

The first question is, how many times has another person messed up your life? The second question is, how many times have you let that same person mess up your life a second time? The third question is, how many times have you let that same person back into your life to, once again, throw your life into turmoil? The fourth question is, why did you let that person into your life in the first place? If they're back into your life, why did you allow them the opportunity to, once again, cause you despair?

It's story time again. I once had an employee, Steve, who was lying and cheating on his work tickets. It came to my attention that this

93

worker was falsifying his service tickets. He was lying about the service hours he was providing and about the amount of product he was installing. The allegations came from one of Steve's fellow workers. But I had to verify the allegations. I did this by contacting the customers he was servicing and asking them how long he was at the work site and what products, if any, Steve had installed. I also visited the various work sites to see if he had actually installed the quantity and type of product he listed on his work ticket. I kept records of his activities for 3 months.

My detective work convinced me that Steve really was lying on his work tickets. There were even tickets where he had forged a customer's signature. I finally confronted Steve with my findings and fired him. Steve, of course, denied all allegations and subsequently filed for unemployment compensation. At my company's instruction, I challenged his claim for unemployment compensation and won. I had too much evidence against him. My company congratulated me on my meticulous detective work. They thought it was great that they didn't have to pay an unemployment claim.

A few years later, that large corporation decided to close its local branch. I went into business for myself, and guess what I did? I hired Steve. Guess what happened? He shafted me again! This time, it was my money he was stealing. Again, he lied about his hours worked and products installed. You would have thought I would have learned my lesson about him from my earlier encounter. I didn't. I wanted to give him a second chance!

In hindsight, I wanted to give myself a second chance, too. I knew Steve wouldn't repeat his past actions. Why? Because I didn't want him to! If you give someone a second chance, they are supposed to show their gratitude for the opportunity you are giving them by

94

performing the way you want them to. Or so I thought. I really don't blame Steve for his actions. I blame myself for giving him the opportunity to cause me anguish a second time.

I'm not saying you shouldn't give second chances, because everyone deserves one. The apostle Paul is the best example of second chances I can think of. He reformed himself from a killer of Christians to a zealot for the Christian cause. But when you give second chances, do so with time, patience and charity. Above all, have the capability to know they just might betray your trust again.

96

Keep It Simple

God doesn't make deals, but how many of us have attempted to make a deal with God? I would wager that 99.9 percent of us have. The deal might be as follows: "Please God, if you would make my spouse come back, I'll be a changed person. I promise I will never mess around again. I'll be kind to my children. I'll come home immediately after work. I won't cheat on my income tax. I'll even be nice to my mother-in-law. I won't drink anymore. I won't beat my dog. Most important, I will give 10 percent of my gross earnings to the church!"

Does any of the above sound familiar? I'm reminded of a movie where the star decides to end it all by swimming out into the ocean. He swims out about 1 mile and has a change of heart. He turns around and asks God for help in getting back. After a few strokes, he tells God he will give up all his worldly possessions if only God will help him make it to shore. At about the halfway mark, he is still asking God for help, but he would like to keep his house and some of his money. With the shoreline in sight, he informs God he really needs to keep his luxury car and most of his money. As he steps ashore, he now tells God he really didn't need God's help after all. The deal is off!

I know a person who suffered a great personal tragedy—the loss of a child. As the child was dying, the parent made a deal with God. If only God would spare his child, he would give him everything! The child did die, and he blamed God for it. He became a very bitter man, not just to God but to everyone and everything around him. That was

98

years ago, and if anything, he has become more bitter and cynical. He still blames God. He has not forgiven nor has he forgotten!

Why would anyone make a deal with God? What material possession do we have that God would want? I can see it now! God wants your Jeep Cherokee 4x4. God will grant your wish if you will only give up your Jeep. Give me a break! We have to remember that in God's playing field, He is the players, the manager, the owner of the team, the owner of the ball field and the city the team plays in. How then, in God's name, can we expect to make a deal with God? Do we really expect God to accept a deal?

Each one of us has a destiny to fulfill. That's the deal God made with us. It's up to us to live up to our destiny the best way we can. I can't tell you what your destiny is. It's up to you to find out. However, there is one destiny that is common to most of us. If we accomplish it, we will make up for many of our shortcomings. It really is a simple thing. Our common destiny is to be good parents! And if you happen to not have kids, then be a good person!

By the way, another really good reason not to make a deal with God is that He often collects. How would you like to have God as the bill collector? Can you imagine telling God the check is in the mail? Can you imagine God giving you a call and informing you that your credit card has been revoked? He wants payment in full NOW OR ELSE! And you know you don't want to know what the OR ELSE is. Talk about stress!

I have a friend who sort of made a deal with God. Howard was sailing with some friends in a very small sailboat off the coast of Massachusetts some years back. They were supposed to be out no more than 3 or 4 hours in very clear weather, or so the weather forecast had predicted. As luck would have it, the forecast was wrong (see

99

cliché, "Never Bet on a Sure Thing.") A terrible storm erupted when they were 10 to 15 miles off shore. It took them about 12 hours of praying, radioing for help, good seamanship and puking to get back to dry land. Howard said that what they mostly did was puke. During one of his many pukes Howard told God, "God, if I get back, I will never set foot in a sailboat again." They did survive and to this day Howard has not even been in the ocean, let alone a sailboat.

When you take a closer look at Howard's statement, you can see he wasn't making a deal with God. He was informing God of what he was going to do if he made it back. Perhaps that is the moral. Don't expect God to grant us our wishes. Instead, ask for God's help in overcoming troubles. God expects us to help ourselves. Ask for God's help, but for God's sake, don't demand it or bargain for it.

"I'm talkin' about peace of mind."—*Tommy James and the Shondelles*

It's up to us to bring our healthiest selves into a relationship!

We all bring baggage from our past experiences into a relationship. Sometimes the baggage is a fine Corinthian leather suitcase without a tarnish, and sometimes it's a raggedy cardboard box.

You and your spouse just had your first child. If you had your druthers, what would you bring your new baby's clothes home from the hospital in, the leather suitcase or the cardboard box? I'm sure you'd choose the leather suitcase. How can we bring no less in our dealings with strangers, fellow workers, acquaintances, friends, family members and loved ones?

Pretend you are a garage sale. People have garage sales to get rid of their junk. Do the same thing in your personal life. Get rid of your emotional junk! If you can rid yourself of your junk, your life's journey

100

toward growth has started. You might even find out you were carrying around an unnecessary, unwanted, heavy and ponderous raggedy old cardboard box!

Put an ad in the paper announcing your upcoming garage sale. It could read something like this: "Huge Garage Sale! Everything must go! No offer will be refused! One of a kind items for sale at rock-bottom prices! Some of the items for sale are pettiness, self-righteousness, envy, meanness, arrogance and boastfulness. All items will be thrown away if not sold!"

Sounds like a great idea for a garage sale to me.

"Elephants and memories are playin' in the band."—*Creedence Clearwater Revival*
Elephants never forget!

Neither do women! This is a topic many male comedians have used to illicit hours of laughter. Women never forget anything! Men, on the other hand, would forget what they had for lunch if not for the food stains on their ties.

Ask a man where his tool box is and his answer will be, "In the basement." If you ask him to be more specific about where it is in the basement, his answer will be, "In the basement. I'll know where it is when I see it!"

Ask a woman where her cosmetics are and her answer will be, "On the third shelf of the linen closet, in front of the iron, next to the toilet paper, with the towels on the other side. Except on the third Wednesday of the odd numbered months. On that day, I clean out the linen closet and put the cosmetics in the bathroom medicine cabinet. The towels go into the spare bedroom closet, the toilet paper I put in the kitchen under the sink, and I always put the iron in the

101

basement next to the tools if I can find them, and I always do!"

In the war between elephants and memories, men don't stand a chance. Elephants are bigger and women remember everything! In the not-too-distant past, the men were off doing important things like protecting their family and property by fighting wars and killing anything in their way. The women had to make sure the family continued to function while the men were away having fun killing and being killed. Men's and women's priorities were and are different!

We are the products of hundreds of thousands of years of evolution. We will continue to evolve, but don't expect change overnight. Be nice to each other!

"Is that you Pig Pen?"—*Peanuts Cartoon*

As sloppy as a pig's pen!

So are men! The quote, "A place for everything and everything in its place" was not written by a man. Being neat is not at the top of any list to most men! Clutter is a way of life for us. You can never tell when you might need something. Why throw away that slightly used 1969 Ford carburetor? You might use it sometime in the next 40 years. Will a man remember where it is? Probably not, but he knows he has one!

Why make the bed in the morning when you will just mess it up again that evening? Hang up your jacket? You are planning to wear that same jacket the next day. Or if not tomorrow surely next week, and if not next week, then at least next month. That would just make added work. If you hung it up, how would you ever find it?

We have all seen front yards with all kinds of junk in them: broken-down cars, lawn mowers, rakes, old refrigerators and 2 weeks of newspapers. I'll bet a man lives there. I'll bet a flustered wife lives there, too.

102

Men are inherently sloppy. It's the result of millions of years of practice. If Sir Alexander Fleming would have been neat and put his head of cheese back in the refrigerator where it belonged after he fixed himself a cheeseburger, we probably wouldn't have penicillin. Good old Alex noticed a mold growing on the 6-month-old cheese and wondered if it was good for anything. Men will eat anything! The rest is history!

Men's and women's thought processes are different. Be kind and tolerant to each other!

"Splish splash I was takin' a bath, along about Saturday night."—*Bobby Darin*
Always put the toilet seat down!

I know, I know, there is no woman on the face of this Earth who doesn't want the seat put down. And I also know that women raise holy hell when they find the toilet seat still up. I guess they have a valid point. I have, on a few occasions, ventured into a dark bathroom, sat down and ended up with my butt in the water. But I was always able to get out. I'll bet that's the answer. The women of this world can't get their butts out once they get them lodged in the toilet! The more I think about it, I know that's the answer! It also solves a personal mystery I've been struggling with these many years.

When I was a wee lad of ten I, by mistake, went into a ladies' restroom at a gas station. What did I see? A skeleton sitting on the toilet, with a purse still clutched in her hands. I'm now sure that poor lady sat down on the toilet with the lid up, got stuck and died. The moral of this story is, men, put the seat down if you want keep your significant other alive. And, I might add, it will make your life easier. Women, don't be too harsh if he happens to forget once in a while. It takes a lot of effort to bend over and put

103

the lid down. I do hope this will be the biggest argument the two of you ever have.

"Instead of breakin' up we should be makin' up."—*The Supremes*

Don't fix something if it's not broken!

If something isn't broken, why would you try to fix it? If something is good, don't fix it, just make it better. An example of this would be a lawn mower with a dull blade. The lawn mower still runs and cuts the grass, but your lawn would look better with a sharp blade, and the mower will last longer.

Improving a dull relationship isn't as simple as sharpening the blade. You can't sharpen only one side of the blade; you need both sides sharp to cut the grass evenly. It'll take two dedicated people to sharpen their blades. You need to work together on the lawn mower project. By working together you will both learn, grow and then teach. Sounds like fun, and it couldn't hurt.

"I thought love was only true in fairy tales."—*The Monkees*

I will never understand women; or I will never understand men!

We aren't supposed to, which is what makes the opposite sex so exciting and at the same time so exasperating. The only advice I can give is to listen without judgment and don't take your partner for granted. We're in the vanguard of an interpersonal revolution that has started in our lifetime. Equality is becoming a reality. Things have changed dramatically. For thousands of years, things were one way. Women were less equal than men. Most men and women were raised to believe in that manner. Oh, it was something that was never spoken,

but every man and woman knew it. The message was given in many subtle ways to both sexes. You don't have to understand the opposite sex but you do have to accept them. Acceptance is the key word. By accepting the differences, growth and learning will occur. Once growth and learning start occurring, the sex really becomes great. Oh yeah, that is an added benefit of acceptance, great sex. What's that I hear from the readers, a willingness to accept, grow and learn? Didn't I tell you learning could be fun?

"Hey little Cobra, don't you know you're gonna shut 'em down."—*The Rip Cords*
    Where you're headed is more important than how fast you're going!

Do you want to continue with the above cliché? Let's see a show of hands. All those in favor of continuing, raise your right hand. All those against continuing, put your right hand down. Hooray, the right hands have it! Let's continue.

Here is a story about my misspent youth. During my 19th year of life, Bill and I were in a smoked-filled pool hall playing nine ball in a town 50 miles from home. Nine ball is a pool game normally played for money, and we were normal 19-year-old kids. That night we were playing the five ball for $1 and the nine ball for $2. It took us 6 long hours and many beers (this place didn't check IDs too closely) to achieve the princely sum, for 1965, of being $25 and some change up.

It was time to leave, but as luck would have it, we weren't playing with other college kids. We were playing with meat packers. Not just mere meat packers, but the actual honest to God killers of the cattle. During the course of the evening we found out just how they would kill the cattle. They used sledge hammers and .22 caliber slugs all administered to the back of the cows' heads. They told us in very

105

graphic detail how they performed their jobs. You could tell they really enjoyed their jobs from the loving way they talked of cattle killing. I learned how they ordained the fatal blow, how they collected the cattle blood, how the cattle bleated and how they strung the cattle up to bleed. Theirs was a running commentary about the best and fastest way to kill cattle during the many nine ball games we played. They supplied us with way too much information about doing away with cows. Some of their stories were really very cruel and inhumane. But we still beat their behinds in nine ball. We hadn't allowed college to interfere with the finer things in life, like pool.

As dedicated college students we had read many of the great novels such as "War And Peace," "Crime And Punishment," "To Kill A Mockingbird," "The Old Man and the Sea," and of course, "Moll Flanders." Those cattle killers couldn't out-quote us, but they did have damn big biceps, and we all know big biceps usually mean little minds.

It finally came time for the cow killers to settle up, but they had a final wager—double or nothing. My friend, Bill, had just bought a new 300 hundred horsepower 390 cubic-inch Ford convertible. Of course, he bragged about how fast his car was to the cow killers during the entire time we were playing nine ball. His bragging occurred during lulls between the killers' bragging about the best way to dispatch cows. The only thing I could brag about was the best way to structure a sentence! When the topics are fast cars and cow killing, sentence structure leaves a lot to be desired!

Anyhow, Bill was telling the cow killers that his 390 was the fastest thing on the face of the planet. His exact words were, "My car is faster than greased lightning!" You should never use that tone with killers. Their reply was, "Prove it, _____hole!"

106

Now, back to that double-or-nothing bet. The cow killers wanted to bet that we couldn't drive the 50 miles between the pool hall in Beadstown, Illinois, and our final destination of Griggsville, Illinois, in less than 45 minutes. There were small towns with stop signs, bridges, hills, curves and nothing but two-lane roads the entire way. My response was, "No way, pay up!" Their response was, "Make us!" Their response won!

We really wanted to win that double-or-nothing bet. Fifty dollars would buy us more than 20 cases of beer and more pool games against docile 1965 college kids.

The rules were that we would start at 11 p.m. sharp from Beadstown. Once we arrived in Griggsville, we were to call the cow killers collect from a pay phone, but only if it was no later than 11:45 p.m. We never discussed how we would collect the money if we won the bet. You know, I think the cow killers had it planned that way! College doesn't offer a course in common sense!

We started the road trip with Bill driving and me riding shotgun. Bill had no fear when it came to driving fast. He thought he was the second coming of Barney Oldfield. But that night Bill even out-did himself. Within 5 minutes, I knew what the term "abject fear" meant. I pleaded with him to slow down or, at least, let me drive. He refused. I then had a brainstorm. I told him we would cheat and call from a town 15 miles closer. The cow killers would never know the difference. Bill refused. His manly virtue was at stake!

After another 5 minutes of absolute terror on my part—we were taking corners on two wheels and running stop signs—I offered to drive. Bill refused. I then did what any sane person would do in a similar circumstance—I lied. I told Bill I was going to puke in his car! Even that didn't stop him. He just drove faster so I could puke

107

in Griggsville instead of his new convertible. I couldn't have puked even if I had wanted to. I was too scared. I continued my charade and told Bill I had to lie down in the back seat, actually the back floorboard. I became one with the floorboard and prayed for deliverance. Bill was driving so fast and the roads were so hilly that we were literally airborne six or seven times. We bottomed out once, and the resulting landing actually dented the floorboard. I know it was dented because the dent hit my nose. I did get even with Bill for scaring me to death. I bled all over his back floorboard from the nose bleed the dent caused.

We finally arrived in Griggsville and called the cow killers. Surprise, surprise! They didn't answer! Bill wanted to go back, find them and demand our money. I told Bill he must have a death wish, and there was no way I was getting back in the car with him. We never saw the cow killers again and, of course, we never saw our money.

We didn't prove a thing that night. Well, yes, we did. We proved just how stupid and lucky we were. We did prove one other thing. The trip between Beadstown and Griggsville can be made in less than 45 minutes. Bill did learn something, too. He learned his car's exhaust system and shocks had to be replaced the next day. They were broken as he was making his airborne landings.

Sometimes the trip isn't worth the experience. But you still must learn from it. I learned that I needed to change the flock I was flying with!

To Ask The Simple Question Is Hard

"We cannot live authentically or responsibly unless we determine our own values, principles, desires and goals—and stand up for them."—*Nathaniel Branden*

Anger is an expression of fear!

Most of the time, anger is what happens when we are no longer in control—mainly emotional control. Take an inventory of the people you know and split those people into two groups—those who rarely get angry and those who get angry on a regular basis. Now, a question: What is the major difference between these two groups? I'm sure you can think of many minor differences, but try to think of a common difference that will separate the two groups. Is it their hair color? No. Is it their educational background? No. Is it the car they drive? No. Is it the part of the world they were born in? No.

Well, just what could it be? Let's think about some more of the major differences. Could it be that they want to be in control of all things at all times? By Jove, I think you've got it. You might have stumbled onto the reason that 97.9 percent of the angry group gets angry. They don't get angry for any reason other than their lack of control. They feel they need to be in control of everything. Once they lose control, they get angry. They are angry on an almost daily basis because there is no way they can be in control of everything and everybody around them 24 hours a day.

When they lose control, they try to regain it by doing something that invariably angers others. When the others lose their composure, the control freak will say, "Who, me? What did I do?" By causing the

other person to lose his temper, the controller is now back in control. That, Dr. Watson, is the way he or she wants it. Remember, they must be in control of everything and everyone.

Let's use an example. You're trying to teach your 14-year-old son fiscal responsibility. You give him enough money, through an allowance, to buy lunch each day at the school cafeteria. At the time you give him the money, you explain the principles of budgeting to him. School lunch, as we all know, isn't great but it's reasonably priced and filling. Your son's friends start going to a local hamburger stand for lunch instead of having the school lunch, and your son wants to join them. He runs out of money for lunch after 3 days and comes to you for additional lunch money. Of course, you ask him why he needs more money? He tells you he's going out to lunch with his friends, and the hamburger stand is more expensive than the school lunch.

Your response is to once again explain to him how to budget. He listens very little. After the budget lecture is over, he again asks for more money. You explain fiscal responsibility to him once again, and you tell him he isn't getting any more money until the following Monday. He immediately goes on in detail about starvation and the poor quality of school lunches. Again, you tell him there will be no more money until the following Monday. The boy is not a happy camper! As an added precaution, you forbid him to ask his grand-mother for any extra money. You tell him not to even discuss it with her! Your mother has horned in on family discipline many times before, and you don't want it to happen again.

About 3 weeks later you overhear a telephone conversation your son is having with a friend. You hear him tell his friend the reason they haven't seen each other at lunchtime is because he has been going to Mac's Place for hamburgers. After he hangs up, you tell him

110

you overheard the conversation and ask where is he getting the extra money for lunch? After a few minutes of beating around the bush, he finally says, "Grandmother!"

For the second time, you again forbid him to ask her for any extra money. You call your mother and explain the situation to her and beg her to please go along with your decision. Her reply is, "But he'll starve and the school food is terrible!" For the tenth time you explain your wish that she please butt out and not to undermine your discipline. Reluctantly she answers, "Well, all right. But I don't like it!" You don't believe a word your mother agreed to. You know how your mother likes to be in control and this is an opportunity she lives for.

Two weeks later, you decide to do some undercover work as a private investigator because your son hasn't asked for any additional lunch money. So you ask him, "How are the school lunches, son?" He replies, "OK, I guess."

You hang out at Mac's Place during the school lunch hour. Guess who shows up? Yep, your son and his friends! You corral your son, and eventually the truth comes out. His grandmother has been giving him the extra lunch money he needed. You are really angry, not to mention really ticked off. You take your son back to school and inform him he is grounded for 3 weeks, and he is never to eat at Mac's Place again. That even includes after school hours. Your son is once again a very unhappy camper.

You drive to your mother's place in a red fog of rage. Your mother is home and you, in a huff, ask her, "What are you doing giving money to my son for lunch?" Her reply is, "I didn't give him money for lunch. It was for his birthday!" You say, "But his birthday is more than 4 months away." She replies, "I know that. It's just an advance." You end the visit being very angry with her.

111

Your mother used anger to get control of your son and to guarantee a place for her in your son's life. Fear is like that. It needs to be in control. Nothing else matters except control. As soon as you realize there is very little you are in control of, that's when you can start gaining control over your life. I know that sounds like a dichotomy, but it isn't. Anger is an expression of control over another's life. Once you realize control over others is impossible, the anger will lose its appeal and, therefore, control will lose its appeal. Man, that really sounds profound, doesn't it?

"A human being's first responsibility is to shake hands with himself."—*Henry Winkler*
Never bet on a sure thing!

When in your life have you ever had something you were so sure of that the thought of failure never even crossed your mind? I'm sure each of you has had such a feeling that there was no way you could lose!

A sure thing could be counting on another person. You knew you could trust your life with that person come hell or high water. And what happened? You probably were disappointed. It could have been a business deal, a relationship, a friendship or a family event. We have all heard the old saying, "The only sure thing in life is death and taxes." I'm positive about death, but I've known and read about too many people who don't pay taxes to place much belief in the tax part.

How about the Wall Street stockbrokers of a few years ago? They had insider information about upcoming sales and mergers. As you know, they made a tremendous amount of money, but got caught breaking the law. So what happened? They were charged and convicted, and they spent a few years in prison. Between their fines and lawyers' fees, they lost most of their money and all of their

112

morals. They bet on a sure thing, and they certainly paid the price. So you see, even insider information isn't a sure thing. Risking a jail sentence isn't betting on a sure thing either.

How about relationships? Most of us have had our hearts broken because of a failed relationship. It can happen in grade school or the retirement home. Things happen. You never have complete control over events. And you certainly can never have control over people!

That is, my friends, what this is all about. How can you ever expect to know the outcome of an event when other people are involved? You can't. But there is a sure thing you can bet on, and that is yourself! You can bet on a sure thing because the sure thing is you. You know the outcome before it happens. You have to believe in and trust in yourself. That's not easy to do. You have to know yourself and be very comfortable with who you are. How do you become trusting and comfortable with yourself?

Few people can know themselves without a personal struggle of some kind (see cliché, "No pain, no gain.") You have to look inward and truly see your soul. Once you allow yourself to do that, you then have the chance to know your soul intimately. You are on the road toward character development! After you have done that monumental task, and only then, can you say, "I can bet on a sure thing and that sure thing is me!"

"Character is built out of circumstances from exactly the same materials man builds palaces, while another builds hovels."—*G.H. Lewes*

People who say, "I don't trust anybody," can't be trusted!

113

Most people who say they don't trust anyone go out of their way to show that they, and they alone, are trustworthy. They normally have a very low opinion of others, and to make up for other's untrustworthiness, they become pillars of truth, justice and the American way of life. Yes, they do become Superman in their own eyes.

Without their guidance their families would crumble. It's only through their diligence that the people around them are able to function and survive. These people are a royal pain in the neck. They are really big into trying to control others. If they could control the length of the days, they would. Constant turmoil with everything and everyone around them gives them great pleasure. What can you do if you are confronted with this type? Absolutely nothing! I just hope you aren't involved with one of these people. If you are, your purpose in this lifetime must be to develop character.

"I'm leavin' on a jet plane. Don't know when I'll be back again."—Peter, Paul and Mary
Never open a window on an airplane!

There are more than a couple of reasons why you shouldn't do this. For one thing, it's dangerous. Why would you want to put yourself in danger? Another reason might be that you would probably really annoy the person in the seat next to you, not to mention the captain, the Federal Aviation Administration, your mother and anyone else you can think of! Also, you just might let a bird into the plane. Just think of the terrible time you would have catching that bird. Birds have a tendency to fly all over the place, emitting white material on everything and everyone while they are flying. Do you know why birds are always emitting as they fly? It's so they don't have to carry any extra weight. I'm really glad that cows don't fly!

For all the above-mentioned reasons, people do symbolically open windows on airplanes. Let me name a few ways people do that: cheating on their spouse; taking drugs; driving too fast; drinking to

114

excess; living beyond their means; maxing out their credit cards; not believing the sign that says, "don't feed the bears;" not asking for directions when they're lost; and going up the "down" escalator. Why court danger? There are enough dangers lurking around without adding yourself to the list.

"Great opportunities to help others seldom come, but small ones surround us every day."—Sally Koch
Never play golf in a thunderstorm!

This isn't quite as dangerous as the open window on the airplane, but the message is the same. You're taking an unnecessary risk. Let's say you are playing a round of golf with a few friends. It starts to rain so you quit before you finish the round. You and your friends know the danger of holding a steel golf club while it's raining. The club could act like a lightning rod, and fried golfers aren't good for anything. You and your friends decide to wait out the rain at the 19th hole.

You're having fun tipping a few brews, lying to each other and laughing with your friends. You look outside and see the rain has set in for the day. Your golfing day is over, so it's time to pack up and go home. However, one of your golfing buddies, Newt, has tipped about ten too many brews. You ask him if he needs a ride home. His answer, "No pro'em, I perfely cable of drivin'." You realize he shouldn't be driving, and you tell him and your friends so! Your friends tell you to leave Newt alone. After all, they say, he only lives eight blocks from the golf course, and he should be able to drive that far. You stand your ground and say, "There is no way I'm going to let Newt drive in his condition. I don't want it on my conscience if something should happen. I'm going to drive him home with or without your help!" Your friends continue to tell you, "It's no big

115

deal, he can do it." You are determined and once again state your belief. "We quit playing golf because our chances of getting hit by lightning was 650,000 to 1! Newt's chances of driving home without incident are a lot less than that!"

You physically take Newt's car keys from him. You shame another friend into following you to Newt's house and driving you back to your car.

You wonder if your actions averted a tragedy. You'll never know and that's the beauty of it!

"My upbringing is filled with inconsistent messages."—*Calvin, from the cartoon "Calvin and Hobbes"*
Don't live your life through your kids!

This does disservice to everyone concerned, both the kids and their parents. My daughter competed in track and field. She started running when she was 10 on the club level. She ended up being an All–American runner at the University of Florida. From the very beginning of her running career, she competed against other runners whose parents were openly critical when their offspring didn't live up to the parent's expectations.

I'm reminded of two parents in particular. One was a mother whose daughter ran for a competing track club in another town. The other was a father whose daughter ran for the same club as my daughter.

The mother would literally run in front of the stands, yelling and screaming at her daughter while her daughter was competing. After the race was over, the mother would tell her daughter everything she did wrong during the race. She did this in a very loud and belittling voice that the entire world could hear. You could tell the daughter was very embarrassed at the way her mother was acting. We found out a

116

few years later, after the daughter was in high school, that she had told her mother she would quit running if her mother continued behaving in such a loutish manner.

They compromised. The daughter would continue to run, and the mother would not attend any of the track meets. The daughter truly enjoyed running and the competition, but her mother took the joy of the sport away from her. The daughter was able to confront her mother about what was important to her, which was the joy of competition! That confrontation took a lot of courage on the daughter's part. I will say this for the mother, she listened and agreed.

The father, on the other hand, was not openly verbal. Whenever his daughter ran, he always sat very quietly. It wasn't until after the race that he would voice his displeasure. No matter how well his daughter ran—and she was a national champion—there was always something about her performance of which he was critical. This went on for years. Finally the daughter, during her junior year in high school, moved out of the house to live with her grandmother in another city. To this day the daughter and father aren't on speaking terms.

In both cases, each parent set expectations that the daughter could not possibly live up to. The father became very bitter because his daughter could not perform in the superwoman role he wanted, while the mother was willing her daughter to be supergirl through sheer lung power.

Our children are our most precious asset. We should treat them as such. We owe it to them to treat them with the respect they deserve and the respect we as parents deserve. Our children are a part of us. Not showing them respect is akin to treating ourselves with disrespect. By respecting your children, you give your children a head start on the road of life.

117

"At the touch of love, everyone becomes a poet."—*Plato*

Always fix a slow leak!

This one is a really easy saying to figure out. If you don't fix that slow leak, you will eventually have a flat tire or a failed relationship. But it does take more than one person to fix a tire. First, you have to know the tire is leaking. Second, you have to take the tire off, put the spare on and then have the garage repair the tire.

Sometimes the tire will have to be replaced because you let that leak get bigger and bigger until you ruined the tire. If it's ruined, the garage can't repair it. The garage probably told you it could have been repaired if the leak was caught in time. But n-o-o-o-o-o, you didn't take the tire in for repair at the time you first noticed the slow leak. Someone probably pointed the slow leak out to you, but you were too busy to do anything about it, right? Did you think the leak would fix itself? You would have done anything to save that tire, right? Does any of this sound familiar?

Sadly, this happens all too often. Can we do anything about it? Well, for starters, both drivers of the car need to check the tires to spot any slow leaks. If they see any, they need to repair that leak before the tire is ruined. That sounds easy enough, doesn't it? It *is* easy if both drivers believe in the maintenance of their tires. Remember, fix that slow leak before you ruin the tire! Don't let it get to an irreparable condition.

"I know this love of mine will never die."—*the Beatles*

Always expect things to break the day after the warranty expires!

This only applies to things mechanical, not to people. This is really a very negative approach to life and shouldn't apply to concerned and

118

spiritual individuals. The main reason things break is because the people who own them don't maintain them properly. They expect things to last forever without maintenance. This is also true with relationships.

Relationships have to have the proper maintenance to ensure you'll get a lifetime of service from them. You've all seen the television commercials where car owners testify to getting many years and hundreds of thousands of worry-free miles from their car or truck. The commercial wants you to believe that years of service and thousands of worry-free miles is because of that particular model. But it's really because the owners maintained their vehicle properly. If you want years of worry-free service from your relationship, you have to maintain it. Go in for the 5,000 mile check-up! Do that and your relationship warranty will never expire. Just think—a lifetime guarantee! With no trade-ins!

"People who need people are the luckiest people."—*Barbra Streisand*
Roll with the punches and hang onto each other!

"No man is an island." "No man can stand alone." "We need people!" It's the rare individual who can achieve awareness, growth, learning and understanding without the benefit of others. Perhaps there is a hermit living alone on a mountaintop who can affect the change our society needs, but I doubt it! Change requires commitment, dedication, love and above all, humor.

There are many wrongs we need to start righting. We can right the wrongs! But we need to do it together. We need people who need people! Start with your family and carry on from there. During the writing of this book, I listened to hours upon hours of songs, mainly songs from the 1960s. I also wanted to listen to country, but I couldn't. I don't own a hound dog, a pickup truck or a cowboy hat. The radio

119

would shut off automatically after 10 minutes. I was amazed at the number of songs talking about love, relationships and commitment. I'm convinced that if we cultivate each other, we will grow and learn. This growth process can lead us into a sphere of spiritual awareness other worlds can only dream about. Go out there and "be all you can be." Now there's a motto the Army should consider using.

"Listening, not imitation, might be the sincerest form of flattery."—Joyce Brothers

You can't plow a straight line by looking behind you!

This is another old farm cliché that's based on truth. If you continue to look behind you to see where you've been, you won't be able to see where you are headed. And knowing where you are going is very meaningful. You won't be able to plow a straight line. And a straight line in farming is very important. If the line isn't straight, planting, and eventually harvesting, will be very difficult. I most assuredly understand what this cliché means, because I once worked for a very patient man who happened to be a farmer.

During my freshman year in college, I elected to quit school early, in March. My grades weren't what they should have been. (I didn't allow college to interfere with my education.) My parents thought it would be in my best interest not to further my social education until I could also further my college education. A friend of mine was leaving for 6 months of National Guard training, and his father needed someone to help him on his farm. I asked for the job, and the unsuspecting farmer gave it to me. I'm sure he's still telling stories about my ineptness 30 years later.

It was like a Three Stooges movie from the first day of my short-lived farming career. Anything I could possibly do wrong, I did! On

120

my first day of work, he asked if I knew how to plow, and I very confidently said, "Of course!" He told me to cultivate his nearby cornfield. A cultivator is a piece of machinery with nine forks that attach to the back of a tractor. It's supposed to dig out any weeds between the corn rows. He asked if I had any questions. I didn't want to appear stupid, so I of course said, "No." He then left me to my devices. The only problem I had was, I wasn't able to tell a corn plant from a weed. Mr. Farmer returned in about 2 hours to a very weed-free cornfield. It was also a very corn-free cornfield! Things got worse from there.

My next adventure was helping Mr. Farmer drive cattle from one field to another. My job was to make sure the cattle took the east gate and not the west gate. It was a very simple assignment. Once the cattle were through the east gate, all I had to do was close and bolt it. Mr. Farmer was driving the cattle toward me. I opened the gate, the cattle ran through it, and I closed it. I did my job! As Mr. Farmer approached me he starting yelling, "@#*&^#%!?" It turns out I had opened the west gate by mistake. I turned around in time to see the cattle loping down the country road that ran parallel to the field. It took us the rest of the day to catch those fugitives.

He decided to give me another chance with his tractor and plowing. Wrong choice! He put me atop a big 880 Oliver diesel with the instructions to plow the north 40 in third gear, but to slow down and raise the plow every time I drove across the grass waterway that ran the length of the field. Mr. Farmer once again asked me if I had any questions. Being the intelligent person I am, again I said, "No." I actually did as he instructed for the first hour.

But driving a tractor is very boring. There is nothing to do except look at dirt and more dirt. I wanted to get this job over with as soon as possible, and Mr. Farmer was nowhere in sight. I put the tractor in

121

fourth gear and engaged the overdrive. I was really moving. I estimated I was going to finish the plowing in half the allotted time. Things were going marvelous. The dirt was flying, the birds were singing and I wasn't bored. Then, I approached that evil grass waterway. Mr. Farmer's directions to slow down and raise the plow upon entering the grass waterway never crossed my mind. I was on a roll! As I exited the waterway, I noticed the tractor had slowed down and was lurching to the right. I looked behind me to see what was the matter.

In a matter of seconds, Mr. Farmer's instructions became crystal-clear. The $2,000 plow was in evident distress. In fact, I had broken the heck out of it! The plow was in about eight pieces! I stopped the tractor, got down and surveyed the damage. Two axles were broken, and the plowing disks were lying in the grass waterway. It was at that time that I saw the tree stump in the grass waterway. I had two choices, run or stay and face Mr. Farmer. I decided to stay—it was too far to hike to the high-way. Mr. Farmer did show up about 3 hours after, as it came to be called, "the great grass bust." He didn't say a word. But his face was beet-red, and you could see little beads of sweat appear on his upper lip. We loaded the damaged plow parts into his truck and drove to the parts store. Mr. Farmer continued his silence for the entire 90-mile round trip. I thought it was in the best interest of my personal well-being to do the same.

My next mission, if I would choose to accept it, was to spread manure. Mr. Farmer knew I couldn't possibly break anything per-forming this task. All I had to do was back the manure spreader into the barn, shovel the manure into the manure spreader and drive the spreader into the pasture to spread it. There must have been 10 tons of the stuff. Needless to say, my first attempt to back the manure spreader into the barn resulted in my hitting the side of it. I broke a few boards, and I did my best to hide the damage.

122

Once again, Mr. Farmer told me to drive slowly while I was spreading the manure. I didn't ask him why, but I should have! After two uneventful trips with the spreader, I knew I could cut the time in half by driving twice as fast—and I did. Here I was, bouncing all over the pasture spreading manure in late April. I was at peace with the world. But the bugs were thick, and they kept hitting me in the back of the neck. I slapped at the bugs a few times but they kept coming back. After five or six slaps I noticed these late April bugs were really juicy! And why were there so many bugs in late April? Then I looked at my hand, then I smelled it. The bugs weren't bugs, they were manure! I was driving so fast the manure was being thrown forward and covering me with the stuff. I slowed down.

Part of the agreement I had with Mr. Farmer was that I would eat lunch with his family. The manure adventure happened in the morning. Lunch was yet to come. Normally lunch was a leisurely event. But not this time. It really was kind of funny, watching his wife and two daughters trying to eat their food while smelling me at the same time.

One day Mrs. Farmer asked if I would cut the grass. She said I should be very careful around her prized petunias. She asked if I had any questions. I told her, "I know how to cut grass!" I should have asked her what petunias looked like. The look on her face as I was making the final cut still gives me nightmares. She never talked to me again.

The final Mr. Farmer episode came to be called "the great pig escape." We were separating the sows from their piglets by building pens in the barn. After the pens were built, we started herding the sows into the pens from the front to the back. I never did understand why we did it that way and not from the back to the front. I should have asked more questions. The pig herding went exceedingly well until the last sow. Mr. Farmer had me in the lead, and he was the follower.

123

We were shooing the last sow into her pen when the sow looked at it, turned, looked at me, and said, "Oink." I should explain the sow probably weighed 400 pounds, and the space between the pen and the barn wall was only about 3 feet. There wasn't a snowball's chance she was going into that pen. I stood between her and her chance at freedom. She started her charge and I, of course, did the only thing possible. I placed one foot on the pen, the other foot on the barn wall and stood up. I let the sow run under me! There wasn't enough time, however, to let Mr. Farmer know the sow was coming. I turned around just in time to see the sow try to go between Mr. Farmer's legs. Mr. Farmer couldn't spread his legs enough for her to pass under. The sow carried him on her back, into the barnyard backwards. He must have ridden the sow that way for more than 50 yards before he fell off into a mud puddle. I'm sorry to say I laughed and laughed, but in private of course. The sow stopped her flight about 30 feet away from Mr. Farmer, turned and said, "Oink," then sneered and ran away!

One week later I informed Mr. Farmer I had found a summer job as an orderly in a mental institution and was quitting. He told me, "I'm really sorry to see you go." I don't think he meant it, as he was smiling when he said it!

My farm experience did teach me to ask for instructions. What's simple to one is Greek to another. I still don't know what a petunia looks like!

"Th-Th-Th-That's all folks."—*Porky Pig*

How did you respond to the different clichés in this book? Did you find none, some or all of them offensive? Did you think it was humorous? Was it a book you couldn't put down, or was it one you couldn't wait to take to the trash can? Did you find it insightful, complete hogwash or somewhere in the middle?

No matter what your thoughts are, they're right! They're right as long as you know why you came to the conclusion you did. What's good for the goose is not necessarily good for the gander. Don't you just love the way I continue to come up with one cliché after another? There are hundreds upon hundreds of self-help and feel-good books on the shelves. Most are telling you, "If you follow my instructions, your life will be transformed to happiness, love and prosperity!" How can they all be right?

Earlier, I mentioned that I had read many different types of books: self-help, religious, psychology, new-age and spiritual. I talked to many different people, each with their own views of life. Each book and person had their own philosophy. I decided I needed to know my own philosophy. I started my personal quest toward growing, learning and teaching.

In retrospect, my journey started, as most journeys do, with pain. In 1988, my 16-year-old son was a passenger in an automobile that was struck by a drunk driver. The accident occurred less than a mile from home while he was on an errand to buy a gallon of milk. He was in a coma for 6 days. Although he survived, he had to be retaught how to walk, eat and think. His days as a college prospect in basketball were over. The recovery process for my son took more than 3 years.

THE BACK PORCH PHILOSOPHER

My recovery process took more than 4 years. Anger and revenge was all I could think of. I was mad at everybody and everything. I wanted revenge against the drunk driver, and I was mad at the driver of the car my son was a passenger in. I was particularly upset with God. Why would God take away my son's athletic ability? I wouldn't be able to sit in the stands and be proud as my son made the winning basket! My sense of humor took a vacation. I needed it back, but I didn't know how!

In the fifth year after my son's accident, within a 1-week period, my company decided to down-size and I was out of a very good-paying job, my stepfather died of a heart attack, I almost lost my mother and my wife of 23 years informed me she wanted a divorce and was moving out of town. I had experienced better weeks.

I had two choices—give up, or learn and grow. I unconsciously started the growing and learning process. I began attending a small predominately black church. I was the token white male, and I became the scripture reader every Sunday. A member of the congregation once asked the Pastor why a white man was reading scripture. His answer was, "Because he can!" It was a unique and beautiful experience. That's where I started learning forgiveness, and learning to let others help you learn. I started becoming aware!

I was a member of this very loving church for 2 years. After two years I knew it was time to move on and seek more truths. I needed to develop my philosophy. More important, I needed to know what my philosophy was. Guess what? It happened! I can't think things out without talking. This book is the result of not being able to think. As I was typing this unextraordinary manuscript, I was talking to myself and I was answering. Heck of a deal, don't you think?

I hope you will have as much fun developing your philosopohy as I did. Good luck with your journey.

126

Your assignment is to become a back porch philosopher. How, you ask? It's simple, just think and write. Take your pencil in hand and do the following:

Now that you've read this book, write down your thoughts and feelings about it.

Now, pick out one of the clichés from the list below and write about it.

Next, make up your own original cliché and do your thing.

You now have three works of art. Send these masterpieces to the address listed in the front of this book to my attention. If we're lucky we'll have a, "Life Is Simple, It's The Instructions That Are Difficult," Book II. Have fun!

"Life is simple, it's the instructions that are difficult."

"A woman's place is in the home; and she should go there immediately after work."

"Early to bed and early to rise makes a man healthy, wealthy and dull."

"Don't count your computers until they're online."

"Never judge a book by its cover."

"Better safe than sorry."

"There is nothing new under the sun."

"A fool and his money are soon parted."

"Two is company, three would be fun."

"Never go to sleep in church."

"Never go down the 'up' escalator."

"Always keep your powder dry."

"My ship finally came in."

"It's easier said than done."

"Don't pick your nose."

"Don't rock the boat."

"Always believe in fairy tales."

"All things come to those who wait."

"You can't see the forest because of the trees."

"All that glitters is not gold."

"Water always runs downhill."

128

"Cleanliness is next to impossible."